P9-CDP-157

Moonshiner's Daughter

Growing Up Poor in the Smokies…
How Did We Survive?

Moonshiner's Daughter

Mary Judith Messer

With Love
Mary J. Messer

Doing Well Now Publishers
Lake Junaluska, NC

Published by
Doing Well Now Publishers
PO Box 919
Lake Junaluska, NC 28745

Copyright © 2010 by Mary Judith Messer.

Printed and bound in the United States of America.

All rights reserved. No part of this book may be reproduced in any form or by any electronic or mechanical means, including information storage and retrieval systems, without permission in writing from the publisher, except by a reviewer, who may quote brief passages in a review.

Many actual names and locations in this memoir have been changed to protect the innocent people involved.

Cover design, interior layout and art direction by Buffy Queen.

All photos are from the collection of Mary Judith Messer.

Messer, Mary Judith, --
    Moonshiner's Daughter: Growing up poor in the
    Smokies...how did we survive?/by Mary Judith Messer

Appalachia/child abuse/domestic violence/memoir/female

ISBN 978-0-578-05420-9

First Edition

This book is dedicated to Brenda Lee.

In Memory of

Beloved husband, William Albert Messer

Beloved son, Steven Dale Messer

Beloved friends, Richard and Lois Queen

Stuart Osland, friend and transcriber

My long time friend and dear mentor,
William M. Donovan, from his little "Bunny"

ACKNOWLEDGEMENTS

Without these people and their open-hearted help and encouragement, this book would not have been possible:

My sons Ricky & David, thank you
for your patience & understanding!

My transcribers and editors Stuart and
Nalley T. Osland and Buffy Queen.

My dear friend Nancy Ferguson
who introduced me to Nalley Osland.

My sisters and brother
who lived with me through this upbringing.

Richard Pelzer, who, like me, went through hell.
Thank you for that Sunday morning talk.

Richard and, especially, Lois Queen,
who I considered to be my other mother.

Robert Morgan and Ron Rash,
for their kindness and encouragement.

PROLOGUE

My life story, which I share with you in the following pages, includes many incidents, some illegal, and many people, some doing criminal acts who were never brought to justice. I have changed the names of most of those involved as well as changed some locations so they won't be able to be identified. I do this for my protection and the protection of the innocent people who were part of my life. I have also changed the names of most of my family members, although both my parents are deceased now and I have nothing to fear from them reading this. I have told the facts and circumstances as best I can remember but sometimes, because so much of this is from my childhood and we moved so much, it may be a little confusing once in a while, but it's not on purpose.

I decided to write this book about my life because I just had to. All my life, I have had this burning in my heart about what happened to me and my siblings and no one had to pay for the crimes. Maybe by getting my story out, I will stop hurting. Even though I only had an eighth grade education, and a pretty spotty one at that, and the thought of me writing a book seemed impossible, I couldn't keep it inside. It poured out of me into a dozen hand-written spiral notebooks with pages crammed with what looked like Chinese chicken scratching. I own a small business located off a curvy mountain road near Waynesville, and during slow times at the store, I would go sit in my car out front and write. I had two early transcribers who had to give up after only a few pages because they couldn't read my handwriting or understand my "creative" spelling. But I finally found a couple who became friends (Stuart and Nalley Osland) and they were able to get it onto a computer disk and I at last had something to work with.

I hope that what I share in my book may help someone. Like Dave Pelzer (*The Child Called It*) and Richard Pelzer (*A Brother's Journey; A Teenager's Journey*), my early life was marked by poverty and brutality, but even so, there was also laughter and loyalty between my brother and sisters, which I don't write about too much.

Because there was no organization like AA back then in Haywood County to help people who have the disease of alcoholism, many, many children suffered from having parents who abused alcohol, as we did. And KARE (Kids Advocacy Resource Effort) and REACH of Haywood which now help abused or neglected wives and children weren't around then either. Looking back, I thank God now that there were some neighbors who took pity on us little children and did what they could to ease our misery and feed us when we were hungry.

Even so, once I got out on my own and later with my sister in New York City and then my marriage to a hometown boy, my life took a more hopeful turn. I feel as if I am strong enough now to tell my story. I am a successful business woman and have two sons and a grandson I'm very proud of.

Life for a little girl who was a moonshiner's daughter has turned out okay.

Mary Judith Messer

FOREWORD

My mother, Lois Queen, called me one day and told me that one of her mother's helpers when we were young children, whom we knew as Mary, wanted to see me again and that she had written a book my mom thought I might want to read. I was more than curious to reconnect with someone from my childhood and drove over to Queen's Farm.

Mary, with her sparkling, light blue eyes and quick laugh, was easy to recognize as the former teenager now grownup who had moved with my family to northern Virginia in the mid-fifties. I found out she had been living in Waynesville for many years, had grown children of her own and had decided to write a book about her early life as the daughter of a moonshiner. Because I loved writing also and because of our early connection, I eagerly took her first draft home to read.

As I read through Mary's manuscript, I was stunned and shocked, but I couldn't put it down. The stories of her harsh life in the mountain coves and beside dusty roads in shacks not fit for living in were nearly unbelievable. Yet, I had gone to one of the same schools that Mary had attended and knew firsthand many of the places and people she wrote about, so her memoir rang horrifyingly true. Right then, I knew that Mary's book should have a wider audience because it spoke so movingly of the effects of poverty and brutality, alcoholism and mental illness, on innocent children's lives. I offered to help her "fine-tune" her manuscript and find that audience.

I asked Mary if I could write the foreword to her book, not only because I had the privilege to edit the final draft of *Moonshiner's*

Daughter and assisted in finding a publisher but because I had a special "Mary memory" of her time with us in Virginia that I wanted to recount. She said yes, so here it is.

One afternoon, in the late spring, Mary, mid-teens, and I, four, were walking home from the grocery store on a sidewalk next to a busy street, minding our own business (as folks used to say). Mary was on the road side with me on the other side of her, holding my hand. She had on a pair of "short-shorts", a cute little top and sneakers. Suddenly, we both noticed a convertible with its top down passing on the street next to us. The man who was driving was staring at Mary like he was hypnotized. His head swiveled around toward us as he slowly drove by. Then, BANG! He slammed into a telephone pole and there was a huge crash! We nearly jumped out of our skin from the noise, but what could we do? Not a thing, we just kept walking. That near accident made a lasting impression on me as a little child and provided me with a crucial lesson in human nature. No, the lesson wasn't to watch where you were going when you got behind the wheel of a car, as true as that is. Nor was it to not walk too close to the curb on a city street. After all, we could have been hit because it happened that close to us. Rather, it really helped me to understand the power a pretty girl in shorts can have over a grown man.

Mary, thank you for letting me be part of your (happy) history. You are loved.

Buffy (Sara) Queen

Moonshiner's Daughter

East Waynesville and Third Grade

This is the true story of a "dirt" poor mountain girl who grew up in the Great Smokies of western North Carolina during the 1940s and 1950s.

My mother and father (pictured above) were both from Madison County, Spring Creek section, but we lived in Haywood County. Both counties were very rural and in the heart of the Appalachians.

My father, Terry Lee Long,(not his real name) was one of twelve children. His mother died when he was only two years old and all the children were given away to people who would take them.

Terry was given to some Coles. I never saw any of my Daddy's people so I know nothing about them. He had a sister named Bonnie in Asheville, North Carolina who sent us a Christmas card one time, but I never met her. I think Cheryl, my older sister, met her, but I'm not sure of that.

This is a picture of my daddy and the woman who raised him after his mama died when he was two. I never met her.

My mother was Emily Rose West (not her real name either) and she was always a housewife and a worker in the fields. Mama's father was living but we kids only saw him once, and we called him Papaw. She had two brothers, one was Paul and one was Zolie. I never knew anything about Grandma and we only met Zolie once. He and Papaw stayed in Spartanburg, South Carolina. Paul lived in Waynesville, North Carolina.

My father had several occupations. He rented fields where he grew his tobacco which he and the whole family worked. When it was time to take the tobacco to the warehouse over in Asheville to sell, Daddy and the owner of the fields would go in together. The owner went to make sure he got his half.

Daddy's next occupation was logging. He would go high into the mountains, cut down the biggest trees, roll and slide them down the steep woods until he got them to the road. There he lifted them

Mary Judith Messer

onto the truck that he had borrowed from a neighbor and then took them to a saw mill to sell. At that time, we never had any kind of equipment to lift the logs so Daddy had to get them loaded the best way he could. He was strong and had massive arms.

He sometimes took those logs and skinned the bark off the oak trees. He got one cent a pound for his bark from the tannery which would extract the dye from the bark for the tanning process of cow hides. Joe, my younger brother, and I were made to go up in the woods with Daddy and he would tie wire around a big bundle of bark for us to pull down the mountain through the woods. We fell down lots of time or ran into the trees getting our load stuck. We cut our hands on the wire causing them to bleed as we struggled to get the bundles of bark loose.

Daddy was also a trapper. He caught muskrats in steel traps he set in the creeks and would skin their hides. He mounted the hides on a thin plywood board and hung them on the side of the shack to dry. Then when they were dry, he sold them.

Daddy's next occupation was closer to his heart. He was a moonshiner who, of course, made whiskey called white lightning. He generally took it to town to sell after he had made a run. He was also a moonshiner who liked it so much because of the rewards of getting to drink all he could, and he did just that! He would go deep into the woods, find a nice level, safe place near a fresh mountain creek and carry his entire big copper still there and set it up. He would get Mama to go to town and buy many bags of sugar and yeast. Then he would go to the old corn mill and have his corn ground up fine and behold, white lightning was on its way.

Mama and Daddy had five children, four girls and one boy. The first born was Cheryl, and then Rose, who died in infancy, then I, Mary Judith, was born, and then came Joe and last was baby Joanie. With this big family you might think our Daddy made a good living especially with all of his endeavors, but I am here to tell you no, no, no! My Daddy worked hard, real hard, but we were very poor because of Daddy's drinking. The white lightning also made him mean, and he beat Mama a lot.

Moonshiner's Daughter

Growing up in Haywood County, we moved from one shack to another. By the time I was eleven, we had already moved ten times and I had gone to five different schools. Most of the shacks we lived in were without electricity and only a few had an inside toilet. The first shack I remember us living in was on the edge of the State Test Farm. It was a white, boarded shack with a long porch. Mama came home from the hospital with Joanie when we lived there and Joe, being a small boy, ran into the field of deep grass. He hid and said, "I ain't the baby no more," and he cried for days. We finally had to drag him back home.

* * *

One of the earliest pictures I have of me, on the right, with my older sister. We looked out for each other the best we could. Notice our little matching dresses, and no shoes.

Mary Judith Messer

I was in East Waynesville School in the third grade, where so many bad things happened. A new year of school was about to start and we were told we all had to get a shot on the first day. I was wild with fear because I had never had a shot before and was so afraid of needles. Cheryl said to me, "Don't be afraid. It will only sting a little." I remember vividly the first shot. Cheryl told me, "Not everyone is going to get a Brown Mule Popsicle, just you." At this I brightened up. Lord, how I loved them Brown Mules. I never got one at school even though they were only five cents. I remember all the other children getting one at recess and my mouth just watered as I saw them put their tongues on that nice chocolate ice cream.

We walked with Mama to school that day and got into a long line down the hall. Each child was waiting their turn for the needle and the closer I got, the more I was shaking. I was almost at the front of the line and I could feel pee running down my legs onto the floor. I didn't have shoes on or I guess they would have been full of pee. And then, it was my turn. Louise Smith was the Haywood County School Nurse. She took hold of my little arm. I said, "Oh, God." I knew she was going to stick that thing in my skinny little arm and I was so scared.

She said, "Stand still, Long" and out came the alcohol and cotton. One rub with the cotton and in went the needle. It didn't just sting a little like Cheryl said; it hurt real bad and I let out a howl, with tears running down my face.

Louise took one look at me and said, "You Judith! Your younger brother never cried one tear. So for this, no ice cream for you, you big baby!"

Not only did my arm hurt, but no treat of that Brown Mule ice cream which I knew would make it all better. As I walked down the hall with tears and snot running down my chin, I saw all the children happily eating their Brown Mules.

All I could do was cry. I cried all the way home with Mama telling me to shut up. Cheryl tried to get me to stop, and Joe made fun of me. I was thinking, *One of these days when I grow up, I will run away, get a job and eat all the Brown Mules I want.*

Moonshiner's Daughter

At school the second day, I got excused from class to go to the rest room. It was on the other side of the building, down the long hallway, out a door and down two short steps. As I came to the last step, this little old man was there. I had seen him before with this long handle broom-mop running it down the hall. He had soot all over his face and on his clothing. I dropped my head when I saw him because I was afraid of him. He looked scary.

He caught me by my arm and said, "Hi. I've been watching you and I know you never eat an ice cream like all the other children. How would you like a nickel so you can get you an ice cream?" He kept his grip holding my arm.

I said, "I need to get to the bathroom and back to class before my teacher comes looking for me."

"Come on now! Want that ice cream? Tastes real good!"

He pulled me to the steps that go down into this real dark room with a dirty dirt floor under the school. All I could see was this big, black, hot thing with fire in it. He led me around the big pile of coal where he had a chair. He sat down and pulled me to him.

I was shaking all over and started to cry. I begged him, "Let me go!"

"You know what will happen to you if you don't be quiet. The teacher will take that big leather strap and beat you good. So, shut up."

He then pulled me onto his lap. He put his hand under my little cotton dress and began to rub me. He did this for about five minutes and I was so scared, I couldn't be still. Then he sat me on the dirt floor and reached into his old dirty overalls and handed me a nickel.

He said, "If you tell anyone at all, you will be beat with that leather strap. You come down here anytime and I'll give you more nickels."

He held me back as he stuck his head out the door to see if anyone was around. Then he quick lifted me up the steps and I ran to the restroom.

When I got back in class, the teacher was taking up the nickels as she did everyday for the ice cream.

Mary Judith Messer

She said, "Okay children. All of you, who are going to get popsicles for recess, put your nickels on your desk."

I was so happy. Finally I would get a Brown Mule. I put my nickel on my desk in the corner like all the other children. My teacher came by my desk and picked up my nickel. She leered at me and at the nickel for what seemed like a long time and then she walked back to her desk.

She said, "Boys and girls. We have a thief in our room. I have looked at the dates of all your nickels and the date on this nickel I picked up off Judith Long's desk was the date of the nickel that was missing from my desk. Judith Long stole my nickel from off my desk. Come up here, Judith. Now, boys and girls, what do we do to thieves in our room?"

All the children hollered out at once, "Spank them!"

I walked up to her desk

She asked me, "What do you say for yourself, Miss?"

I tried to tell her that I did not steal her nickel, but she was not listening and that's when I started crying.

She said, "You never have a nickel to buy ice cream. Why did you steal mine?"

As all the class looked and cheered her on, she grabbed me by the arm and threw me over her desk. The class stood up to get a better look. As I cried, I tried to tell her the nickel was mine. After the fourth lick with that long leather strap, I was on the floor, but she dragged me up again. My thin cotton dress did not save me. She hit me three more licks and I went down to the floor again. She got me by the arm and dragged me to my seat. She picked me up and slammed me down on that wooden seat right on my blistered bottom. She never let me go out for recess that day. I couldn't stop crying, so she made me sit at my desk with my head down on the top. When school let out that day, I couldn't sit on the seat of the school bus. The bus driver came back three times, put his hands on my shoulders and slammed me down in the seat, but I hurt so bad, I just popped back up.

He said, "I'll get the Principal and he'll put you down!"

Moonshiner's Daughter

As bad as it hurt, I forced myself to stay seated. Cheryl tried to help me walk after we got off the bus. At home, Mama looked at my bruised bottom and she got so mad. The next day she went to school. She had a fight with the teacher, a cussing fight, not a hitting fight, although Cheryl told me Mama almost slugged the teacher.

Mama said to her, "If you ever lay a hand on Judith again, I will kill you." I was out of school for seven days.

My Mother's Oats box was full of eggs given by a neighbor. Thank goodness we had neighbors who sometimes helped feed us hungry children.

Mary Judith Messer

Hazelwood School & Lots of Close Calls

Not too long after the spanking incident, Daddy went to the creek, where he put out his steel traps and checked to see if he had any muskrats in his other traps. I tagged along with him when Lucie Ann James, a friend of Mama's, came down to the creek to see Daddy.

Lucy asked, "Terry, can Emily go to the Grand Old Opry with me?"

"No! She cannot go!"

"Please let her go," she begged. "I want to go so bad but don't have anybody to go with me. Please! Please!" She begged and looked as if she was going to cry.

Finally he said, "All right, she can go but you better get her back home in two days and no kind of men fooling around with ya'll, you hear?"

Lucie Ann hurried to tell Mama who had been the one to send her to the creek to beg Daddy to let her go. Lucie Ann and Mama left, leaving Cheryl, the oldest girl, to look after us smaller ones. Mama was back within the time Daddy had told them to be back. She had lots of country records by the stars and Daddy never thought to ask her where she got the money to buy them.

Three days later, Daddy was out in back of the house selling some white lightning to a man who proceeded to spill the beans on Mama. He told Daddy that Mama and Lucie Ann went to Nashville with two men. Daddy got so angry, he snatched up a stick of stove wood and into the house he went. I had my arms full of stove wood which I threw down and ran after him. Just as I ran up the steps behind him, he shoved Mama into the kitchen and slammed the door behind him.

We kids could hear the sound of the blows hitting Mama who screamed as each blow landed on her and then a "thump." We banged and kicked on the door, screaming and crying. He finally came out and we ran into the kitchen where we saw Mama laying under the table with blood in her hair, nose and ear. Blood was all over the floor, table and walls; even the old hardwood cook stove had blood sizzling on it. We children ran all over the kitchen, screaming. Cheryl and I got down on our hands and knees and crawled under the table to our mother. She moved a little.

Cheryl and I each got hold of one of her legs and dragged her to the bedroom, even though she was very heavy. Cheryl got a hand towel, put it in a bucket of water and put it on Mama's face and head where he had beat her with the piece of stove wood. We thought she was going to die.

It was nine days before she could get out of bed. Her face was so black, she looked like a darkie, and the fingers on her right hand were broken. Daddy never took her to see a doctor.

* * *

That beating reminded me of the time Mama did have to see a doctor which Daddy fetched. Mama had this long scar on top of her head. She told us once, "Me and Daddy were in the woods and I was trying to help him log when I was pregnant with Rose. Daddy cut down a tree and he shouted for me to run out of the way. I was in my ninth month of pregnancy and couldn't run fast enough to get out of the way and the tree hit me on the top of my head, splitting it open. Daddy went and got old Doctor Kirkpatrick who sewed up my head without any kind of pain medicine. All the feeling in my head was gone anyway so I couldn't even feel him sewing. I was almost dead for weeks and ran a real high fever. The old doctor came to the shack by horseback every week. That wound left the long scar down the center of my head."

Mary Judith Messer

Mama never mentioned it much, but we never knew why Rose was born dead. I guess her fever caused it. We don't even know if somebody was there to help her when Rose was born, since she never went to the hospital. Us kids always thought that Mama's brain injury from Daddy cutting down that tree was what made her do some of the crazy things she did. We couldn't explain it any other way. Looking back, I realize now that Mama was mentally ill and that wasn't a good thing for the mother of four children in desperate conditions.

* * *

We moved from that white plank shack on the Test Farm to another shack in the Ninevah section of Haywood County. That shack was worse than the other. It sat on the side of a mountain and the outhouse was nearby, just a little way from the shack. We had to carry our water from a small spring down the hill which was a good distance away. This old plank shack was home where some real bad memories happened. We Longs now all switched to Hazelwood school. We had to walk to the school bus stop down the steep hill below the shack. We passed several houses and a store. We had to wait for the bus in front of Mrs. West's house. She had two children, a boy and a girl. Mrs. West was so nice to us little poor children. I will just always hold her in my heart. We were waiting on the bus in the pouring rain and Mrs. West saw us soaking wet Long kids and brought us into her pretty house. She dried us off with a good smelling towel and gave us all some snack crackers and such, all we wanted. She did this same thing over and over when it was cold, raining or snowing. We kids never had snack crackers any other time and we just loved them. I hope we never made pests out of ourselves. Thank you so much, Mrs. West, for your very kind heart. I will never forget you.

I was in school one day and this girl that played with me sometimes had brought this little dark-skinned rubber doll to school. She let me play with it when we went out at recess. I loved it so much I never wanted to give it back.

She said, "If you like it so much, why don't you just keep it? You can take it home with you, if you like."

I began jumping up and down for I never had any dolls to play with. I took my little rubber doll on the school bus and when Cheryl and Joe saw it, they started to laugh.

Joe said, "What in the world are you going to do with that little black doll?"

Cheryl said, "You better throw that thing away. If Daddy sees it you will get beat up."

I said, "No, no! I'm going to keep my little doll forever."

Joe ran ahead of Cheryl and me to get to the shack first so he could tell Daddy about my little rubber doll. As soon as Cheryl and I reached the front yard, Daddy was standing in the doorway waiting for us. I had my little rubber doll in my hands behind my back.

Mary Judith Messer

Daddy came into the yard, reached for my arms and jerked me around. I fell down. When he saw my doll, he snatched it out of my hands. His face was all red.

He started cussing, "Where in the hell did you get this G-- damn thing?"

I was crying my eyes out when he kicked me in the stomach three times. Down the trail he went with my little rubber doll in his hand. I crawled into the house, bent over in pain and vomiting. I tried to watch him through the doorway but was vomiting so bad and crying.

He was back in less than a minute and in his hands was no rubber doll but a switch. He hit me four times on the side of my back and then disappeared around the shack. I had a dark welt on my back for a long time.

Joe said, "Your little rubber doll is down in the shit in the old outhouse."

I went into the outhouse next day and he was right. My little doll was down in the toilet hole with nasty stuff all over it. I left crying and never went back. When I needed to go to the toilet, I would go out the trail past the old outhouse. I will never forget my little rubber doll. Sometime later, the old outhouse got full so Daddy dug another hole and moved the old outhouse over the top of the new hole. Then he put dirt on top of the old hole and my little rubber doll also, never to be seen again.

* * *

One day Daddy put Joe, Cheryl and me up onto Old Pat, our work horse. He told us to ride her up the hill to the shack and he hooked up this chain on Pat to a sled he had left in the barnyard. None of us had ever been on a horse before. Cheryl was in the front of the horse next to Pat's head. Joe was in the middle and I was behind Joe. We all held on to each other. Old Pat started up the steep hill above the old barn. The hill got steeper with each step Pat took. I held on tight to Joe and he held on tight to Cheryl. All of a sudden I felt Joe slipping. Then all three of us slid backwards off

Pat's rump and tumbled down the hillside. That hill was just full of rocks; rocks everywhere. I hit a big sharp rock and it cut my leg and arm. Cheryl hit a rock also. Joe just stood up and looked at us. He laughed his head off till he saw all the blood coming out of my leg, then he said "Old Pat ran up to the house."

I could hardly walk for days. Cheryl and I were all skinned up. What a mess we were. But living out in the country as small children, running wild with hardly any adult looking out for us, when I think back, it amazes me sometimes that any of us lived to see adulthood.

There was life-threatening stuff all the time. For instance, sometime after that horse accident, all us older kids were playing around the old barn. Above the barn, Daddy and the owner of the barn had this electric fence to keep the cattle from getting out in the dirt road. We were playing hide and seek. I ran into the barn loft to hide. Cheryl ran in the stables below. Joe was going to hunt us. We heard him counting: one – two – three. In a short time, he was screaming, "Cheryl! Cheryl!" We knew by his sound, he was in bad trouble. I jumped down, out of the loft and ran around the barn and who was stuck in the electric fence? No one but Joe. His hands would not come off the fence. He was stuck to it like glue.

Cheryl was on the same side of the fence as Joe. She took hold of him to pull him off the fence, and then she could not get loose. Daddy ran out of the tobacco field to see what all the screaming was about. When he saw Joe and Cheryl, he ran inside the barn and cut the electric switch. Cheryl and Joe fell backwards onto the ground. Daddy ran to them. They were just laying on the ground. Daddy started rubbing them both. I was on the other side of the fence, standing there crying, thinking they were both dead. I did not want to crawl under the fence even though I knew that the power was cut off. From that day on, the Long kids never went back around that fence. Cheryl and Joe were both lucky to be alive. God sure was looking out for them.

* * *

Mary Judith Messer

Cheryl was at Hazlewood School one day. In her classroom was her teacher, Mrs. Robb. I don't know why but I think it was just because we were Longs, but Mrs. Robb did not like Cheryl at all. I don't think any teachers or the other children liked us poor Longs. Cheryl got spanked with a wooden paddle over twenty licks. A girl in the classroom said all the children counted the licks.

Cheryl was still crying when school let out. Mama went down to the school the next morning and as Mrs. Robb was getting out of her husband's car, Mama got her by the hair. I was scared to death that the much taller Robb was going to hurt my Mama, but Mrs. Robb's husband jumped out of his car and he broke it up by shoving Mama back. Mama was so mad, she was crying. "If you ever touch one of my children again, I will cut you up in little pieces," Mama yelled at her. Cheryl was in very bad shape for a long time. She never went back to school the rest of the year.

* * *

Mama had found a wise way to make more money. She and Daddy sometimes used to go into the woods, no not to make moonshine, but to hunt herbs. They dug ginseng, May apple roots and other herbs, dried them out and sold them by the pound in tow sacks.

"Well," Mama said one day, "Children, we are going to go and gather all the poison oak and poison ivy leaves we can get. Everyone now go down to the barn and each get a tow sack. I want each of the four of you to fill a sack."

I said, "Cheryl, it won't take us long because down behind the barn on the old fence, poison oak is everywhere."

We all took our sacks and spread out to pull poison oak and poison ivy. Within a half an hour, Cheryl, Joe and I had our sacks full. Joanie had only a few leaves in her sack so we all had to pitch in and help her. We showed Mama and she was real proud of us.

She said, "Take all the sacks and empty them in the back of the barn loft. Pour them out and spread them so they can dry. You know how your Daddy and I spread out the roots. Fix these leaves the same."

We did as Mama said because we wanted her to be able to make lots of money. Before night fall, we were scratching all over. Mama put us one by one in this old galvanized wash tub where she did her washing.

"Wash and scrub yourselves real good with that lye soap I made."

First came Joanie, then Joe, Cheryl and then me. But, my Lord, the next morning I could not even see Mama trying to get me up, my eyes were swelled shut. What a mess, and I ached all over my whole body.

Cheryl, Joe and Joanie were no better. We were all a mess. Mama had us build a fire under her old iron wash pot outside. In spite of our bad shape, we had to carry water from the spring down the hill and fill up the old iron pot like we always had to do when wash days came. We filled the pot full and when it got hot, she filled the old galvanized tub and had us pour in some cold water, then ordered us to get in and scrub real good or she would scrub us herself. We did not want her to do that, for when she scrubbed the clothing on the old wash board, she scrubbed!

We did as we were told, but the bath did not help, it only made our raw and itching skin worse. Joanie and Joe walked around crying. It was a good thing school was out for the summer. I would never have wanted the kids at school to see me. They would surely have made fun and this time made fun of my face, legs and arms. This time it would not be my clothing or shoes like they always made fun of.

Mrs. Blaylock, who lived down the hill in this nice green house, saw us standing beside the old dirt road the next day and asked us, "What in the world is wrong with all of you? What's that on your face, arms and legs? Have you got some kind of disease, or what?"

We told her, "No, we got poison oak."

"My G--! Have you been to see a doctor?"

"No. Daddy and Mama got no money."

Mary Judith Messer

We went back to the shack and Mrs. Blaylock came up with some tubes of some kind of salve.

"Here Mrs. Long, put this salve on them every day and if you run out let me know and I will get more at the Smith's Drug Store. You better pray that poison ivy doesn't get in the children's blood. As bad as it looks, they may already have it in their blood."

We children kept playing in the old barn loft and every day we were getting poison oak on us all over. Mama would tell us, "If you don't stay away from the poison oak, I am going to have your Daddy whip you." We could never get rid of that poison oak. We had it all over us and, no, Mrs. Blaylock was never asked to go and buy us any more salve.

One day, Mama went into the old barn loft to see if her May apple roots were getting dry and to spread them out better. That evening, even though she had not been near poison oak, she had it all over her, too.

Mama said, "You kids, take the tow sacks and get in the barn loft, rake up every dried leaf of that poison oak and put it in the sacks."

With the sun shining on the tin roof of the barn, it got really hot and made the poison oak get on us again. It had been in the loft ever since we had poured it in there and you guessed it, we had poison oak all over our body. All except Joanie, she was at the house with Mama. Mama had us kids beg Daddy for some money so we could get some poison oak salve. He finally gave in and gave us two dollars to get it. We took the poison oak in the tow sacks and poured it in the creek. It took weeks before the poison oak was gone. It was a long time before we got better. It was over half the summer.

Why would a mother have her children gather up poison oak? We never found out. I guess she just wasn't thinking straight, again.

Moonshining and Working Tobacco

Daddy was always in the woods. He had Mama go to town to buy lots of sugar and yeast when he was going to start another run of white lightning. He would stay days and nights at a time in those woods. One day Mama needed him real bad. She told Cheryl and me to go fetch him. We all knew where his still was for we were made to help carry in sugar and corn meal lots of times. Cheryl and I were getting near where the still was, when a bullet slammed into a tree just above our heads.

Cheryl called out, "Daddy!"

He was hiding behind this big log. He jumped up and came running out, shouting, "What in the hell are you doing coming up here like this? I almost shot you! From now on, let me know who you are or you will be killed."

"Mama wants you, Daddy," was all we could manage to say.

* * *

Every summer growing up, Daddy had us all working in the tobacco field, all except Joanie. She would step on the small plants and get in trouble. So mainly Cheryl, Joe and I had to plant, hoe, and sucker the tobacco.

Daddy took Old Pat, our horse, and plowed between the rows. Then Daddy put sodium to side dress it. The tobacco was up over my head and it sure looked pretty every year after Daddy got finished with the plowing. After the plowing, he would do a run of moonshine and he would send Mama to town to buy him some fruit jars and lids. He put his moonshine in the jars and took them to the tobacco field. Then, with some post hole diggers, he would make a nice round hole, put a jar of moonshine in and dig another till all his moonshine was safe in the ground. I had to carry his jars to him down the rows of tobacco.

One night around midnight, Daddy woke us all up talking real loud and we heard the sound of him loading his old shotgun. We all jumped out of our beds to see what was going on.

The old shack just had one window in the back. It also had three windows in the kitchen. We ran to the back window. We could barely make out Daddy standing in the shadows behind the shack. Then we noticed just what he was watching. Some flashlights were bouncing their beams all over his tobacco field.

All the sudden that old shotgun went off, "BOOM!" We almost jumped out of our skins. Then we heard him load it again. "BOOM!" This happened again and again. Finally he came in the house after the fourth boom, and said that John Curly and Wade McDaniel won't be back. It was the Haywood County Sheriff and his deputy he was talking about.

The next day when we got up, Daddy had gone back to the woods. He was in the woods for twelve days. Mama said she thought he was afraid to come down out of the woods because the law might be watching for him. All he was living on all those days was his moonshine. He was so crazy, we children never wanted to go to him. We were afraid of him.

He finally came out but was drunk, a sick drunk, and looked like a hillbilly. He was bare down to his overalls, and dirty. My Daddy was a mess.

Not long after he came out of the woods, he went to town for some reason. He was gone almost all day. When he came back, we could tell by the way he was walking, he was drunk.

We were playing in the red clay dirt in the yard. As he got closer to us, he bent down and picked up a rock. Cheryl and I jumped to our feet as he entered the shack.

I ran to the door as he closed it in front of me and it knocked me back into the yard. Cheryl and I ran to the kitchen window but the old window was dirty so we could not see but we could hear them in another room.

We all ran around the shack crying. We got to the side door and it was real high so we could not see in for the door had no steps, just a high door over our heads. We heard Mama screaming as Daddy's blows made a sickening sound.

We picked up rocks, old shoes, bottles, sticks, anything we could find lying around outside and threw them through the door. He beat Mama's head bloody, her face and eye was black and blue for a month. We later found out someone in town had told him that when Mama had gone to town to buy his sugar, she was in a car with some man.

* * *

In the fall of every year, Mama had us children help her go around to all the black walnut trees we could find and pick up the walnuts and help her take off the hull so she could dry them. That old black walnut juice would get on our hands and it wouldn't come off for days. We just hated that black juice. We would spread out the walnuts to dry. When they were good and dry, she would drag out her old iron, put it between her legs, take a hammer and crack the walnuts. She would crack out large kernels. No one could crack out big kernels like my Mama. We tried to help her crack them out, but she stopped us right away. "You are breaking up the kernels," she would say.

She took the kernels after she finished cracking them out and would spread them on a white piece of sheet to dry, then put them in this flour sack. When she went to town, she would take them to Clyde Ray's Supermarket and sell them by the pound. Then she took that money and got us what Christmas we had. She'd buy nuts, oranges, stick candy and cakes and maybe a toy. This was the best time of the year.

One Christmas day was a day to remember for sure. Mama had killed a chicken and she had a large pot of chicken and dumplings bubbling on the stove. She had used her walnut money to

Mary Judith Messer

buy a big chocolate cake and also a coconut cake. She set it all on the table with her big, round biscuits. We couldn't wait for the feast!

As we sat down at the table, Daddy started talking foolish about something or other. He was drunk, as usual. Mama tried to settle him down to get him to eat something. Every minute he got louder, cussing and mumbling. Then all at once, he jumped up and grabbed the old shotgun. A shot went off and we four children ran out the door, Mama right behind us. It was freezing, and we ran out without shoes, or coats. We ran up the hill to the old gravel road and then ran down through Ninevah, my feet numb and my teeth chattering; I was so cold. Cheryl had no coat or shoes either and Joanie was crying, being carried on Mama's hip. Joe was almost crying. We ran way down the gravel road. We crossed over a big wire fence, down a hill through a cow pasture and into an old barn.

We crawled up in the loft of the barn into some hay. Mama made a hay bed for Joanie, put her in it and pulled hay over her. Then she laid down next to us and got as close to us as she could. I lay there all night long, starting at every little sound, afraid it was Daddy coming to shoot us. My stomach was growling for all our good food we left. Joanie was sobbing and Mama put her hand over her mouth because she was afraid Daddy would come to hurt us if he heard Joanie. Mama finally got Joanie to stop crying. It was almost daylight; in spite of being cold and hungry, I had finally drifted off to sleep.

Mama woke up and she whispered real quiet, "Let's go and see if he has slept it off."

We all eased out of our safe place in the hay. Joe's lips were blue from the cold. I was shaking in my cotton dress. What a night! We stumbled and fell lots of times before we got up to the road. Joanie was on Mama's hip and she fell once. When we finally got to the old shack, the door was wide open and there was not a sign of Daddy. All the windows in the kitchen were blown out. Glass was everywhere and I mean everywhere, including in all the food. The old iron stove heater was out and so was the old wood cook stove. The shack was like an ice box. It was no warmer than outside. Mama had Cheryl and me carry in some firewood. When we walked

Moonshiner's Daughter

out, Cheryl and I both cut our feet. Mama tried to sweep up all the glass. The coconut cake was on the floor in little pieces. Joe tried to get some food but Mama stopped him for he would surely die if he ate any of the glass. Even the plates were full of glass.

Mama said, "Daddy must have run after us with the gun. When he saw we had run away, he turned around and shot out all the windows. He's probably back up in the woods." We knew that was where Daddy had his still.

Mama and Cheryl nailed pasteboard over the windows to try and keep out the cold. It didn't really do much good. All the ruined food was put down the hole in the outhouse.

Of course, Daddy came back. Merry Christmas.

* * *

I remember one day Daddy had Cheryl and me working in his tobacco field. He gave both of us a long handled tobacco knife that was curved so we could whack down a stalk. Then we would take the stalk and pull it down over the piercing point called a spud, which was very sharp, that Daddy put on the tobacco stick so the stalks of tobacco would slide down the wood stick.

I was in one row cutting and Cheryl was in the one next to me. She pulled her hand back, the one holding the tobacco knife, and whacked right into her leg and the blood started gushing.

I screamed as loud as I could, "DADDY!"

Daddy came around the field with Old Pat pulling a wood sled. As he came to where we were working, he shouted at us, "What's all the racket?"

He saw Cheryl's leg and quickly grabbed hold of her dress and tore off a piece of cloth and put it in the big gaping hole of her leg. "Hurry, take her to the house. Help her now!"

In spite of blood running down her leg, Cheryl and I climbed up the steep hill above the old barn to the shack. Mama was in the yard bent over her wash board. The rag on Cheryl's leg had washed off, from all the blood, and the big gash in Cheryl's leg gapped wide

Mary Judith Messer

open. Mama took one look and fainted over on the ground. Mama would always faint over when one of her kids was hurt and bleeding.

Cheryl and I went into the shack, got some rags, put them in the gaping gash on her leg and tried to stop the bleeding. It kept soaking through the rags. After we tore up two full sheets, the blood finally cleared up a little, but it was still bleeding. We went to the yard with a wet towel and put it on Mama's head because she was still out cold. Finally she came to. No one took Cheryl to the doctor. Mama just put something called Rosebud Salve on her leg for days. To this day, Cheryl has this wide scar on her leg.

Daddy never put a tobacco knife in our hands again, but we always got a hoe put in them. We had to hoe tobacco, corn and everything, all day long. In a way, in spite of the teasing and whippings I got there, I thought *I would be better off at school.*

All of us kids in the tobacco field with Daddy. He was a real good tobacco grower. We tried to help all we could but it really wasn't a job for children and my sister had the scar to prove it.

Moonshiner's Daughter

Miss Nettie, the Court House & Lions Club

Daddy was in the woods for over a week one time, not in the part of woods where he had his still, over on the left side. I guess he was up there on a big liquor drunk.

We were playing in the yard when all at once, we heard shots "bang out" in the woods. They came from all directions. Daddy was shooting at the law, again. I guess they were after him.

After fifteen minutes, all was quiet, and we went on with our playing. We scampered down the hill to the old barn and climbed up in the loft, then jumped out, swinging on the poles inside like little monkeys. We had such fun.

From the high loft, we could see across the dirt road to an old house of gray planks. The porch was almost falling down the bank. That shack looked like the wind would blow it down at anytime. We kids thought nobody lived in it. It's not that it was so different from what we lived in, it wasn't, but it had all these old vines all over and we knew for sure that it was full of poison snakes. We would never go across the road and up the bank to look it over. It was too scary looking.

Cheryl and I were looking out the open barn loft door toward that old shack when slowly the door started to creak open. We were so scared; we just stared with our mouths open. What stuck its head out, but this old black woman.

We were so scared of the sight of her, we were shaking. We scrambled back into the barn so she wouldn't see us. Joe and Joanie saw her also, and, of course, Joanie started to cry. We four hide back in the barn.

That was the first black person we had ever seen. Her hair was white as snow and she had this rag tied around her head with her hair sticking out all over. She had on a real long old dress that touched the ground so you couldn't even see her feet.

Cheryl and I peeped through the cracks in the old planks and watched her hold on to a post under her old porch. She was trying to get down the steps, holding a broom in her hand.

We wondered if she would come after us with that thing.

She finally got down the old steps onto the dirt yard that didn't have one single blade of grass on it. Then she did something that amazed us. She started sweeping all over her dirt yard. We stayed hidden in the barn till she hobbled back up her old steps and into her house. The door shut, and then we slipped out of the barn loft and ran up the hill to our shack as fast as we could go.

When finally we caught our breath, and told Mama about the old black woman, she just laughed and said, "You have just seen Miss Nettie Tucker, the little lady in that house across from the barn. She will not hurt you." Then I remembered my little black rubber doll Daddy threw in the outhouse.

When we did go to play in the old barn, we would look for her. It was a long time before we saw her again. She came out one day when we were told to go put some hay down out of the loft for Old Pat. Cheryl and I had our arms full of hay as we came down the ladder at the back of the barn. She was in her yard with her broom.

We stopped dead in our tracks for she just stood looking at us, with our arms full of hay.

Cheryl said, "What is she going to do to us?" I was too scared to talk. Then after a few minutes, Miss Nettie put up her hand in greeting.

Without thinking, Cheryl and I, at the same time, threw our hay down; we both put our hands up at her at the same time. From that day on, we tried to come to the barn just so we could see Old Miss Nettie and get to wave at her. We never saw her much but we always looked for her.

* * *

Moonshiner's Daughter

Down the road across from our tobacco field and below Nettie's house was a rock building. It was McCracken's Store. We never got to go in the store, but up on a little hill above that store, we found a trash pile where the McCracken's dumped all their trash.

Cheryl, Joe and I slipped up that hill and found the trash pile one day. It was piled up with all kinds of things. We found lots of boxes of Almond Joys and Mounds candy bars all dumped out. We were in candy heaven. We found us an empty box and filled it with all the candy we could carry. We ate candy for days and we had never had it so good, until all four of us got sick and started vomiting. After that, I never wanted any Almond Joys or Mounds candy bars again. I think the candy was moldy.

One day Mama told us that the Blaylocks had gone up to see their people in Virginia for a few days. Yes, this was the same Mrs. Blaylock that went and bought the poison oak salve for us. Mama told us to go down to the Blaylock's house and climb in the window and get us some of their pretty clothing and any nice things we wanted.

All four of us kids went down the hill to the nice green house. Sure enough, we found we could raise the bedroom window. We got a bucket to climb on and get in. I thought *what a nice house.* The beds had nice covers and bed sheets and all. The house had an inside toilet. The whole house was nice with pretty rugs even on the kitchen floor. I thought *if only I could live in a house half this nice, I would be in heaven.*

In the kitchen, we ate all kinds of crackers, little round orange-colored ones called Ritz and flat, brown ones called Graham crackers. We ate till we almost burst. Joanie took a box of crackers and we let her out the door. She went home. Joe, Cheryl and I got our arms full of clothing.

The Blaylocks had two teenage girls that were larger than Cheryl and me. Mrs. Blaylock was a heavy woman and our mother was much smaller than her. But at the time, we never gave a thought to who could use their clothing. Not a thing could we wear. I guess Mama never thought much about that either when she told us to get

Mary Judith Messer

us some pretty clothes. We three got home with all the things; we just piled them up in the corner of the bedroom in the shack.

One day soon after, Mrs. Blaylock showed up at the shack and was talking with Mama, when we got into the yard after school. Mama told Mrs. Blaylock, "I am going to give Cheryl, Joe and Judith, a good belting! You kids get into the shack and take all those clothes back to Mrs. Blaylock's house, right now!"

We did as we were told, but Mrs. Blaylock said she would have to wash them good to get the bed bugs out before she and her girls could wear them again.

When we got back home, Mama called Mrs. Blaylock *a bitch* and other bad cuss words and that was all that was ever said about that. I hated to make enemies with Mrs. Blaylock for she had been nice to help us when we had all that poison oak.

* * *

One real cold winter night, we had all gone to bed, leaving Daddy sitting at the kitchen table drinking his moonshine and talking to one of his men customers. The price was $2.50 for a quart, $5.00 for a half gallon. The man bought a quart and then left. Daddy started talking to himself, getting louder every minute and he woke me up. I knew by the way he sounded that he was getting madder and madder. Before long he was cussing Mama from the kitchen, even though she was over in her bed across from us four children's bed.

He got so loud that Cheryl, Joe and Mama woke up too and we all scrambled out of bed and on our feet. Mama tried to get Joanie up. I grabbed a sweater for I had no coat. I did get my shoes on. Cheryl was trying to find her sweater and shoes in the dark without Mama lighting the lamp.

Mean and drunk on white lightning, Daddy staggered into our room. He grabbed Mama by the hair and she fought to get loose, but Daddy was lots taller and bigger. Mama, Cheryl and I hit him as hard as we could and Joe had him by one of his legs. He punched Mama square in the mouth and she had blood coming out of her mouth and

Moonshiner's Daughter

nose. She twisted out of his grip, he fell down and we all headed for the door. She had lost her front teeth but we got away. We ran down the hill past the old barn and on down past the rock store. We continued to walk as fast as we could.

Mama walked us all the way to Waynesville to the Court House on Main Street. The streets were deserted at that time of night which was probably good. What a sight we made-- a poor woman, bleeding from her mouth and nose, blood all over the front of her dress, dragging four little shivering children behind her. We walked up the wide sidewalk leading to the entrance and Mama pulled on the big carved door and it opened, much to our surprise. We went inside, so grateful it was nice and warm. Cheryl was frozen for she and Joe did not get a sweater or shoes. Mama lead us back into this huge building where we found some long wooden benches. We each lay down on one and finally fell asleep. The next morning before anyone came into the Court House, Mama woke us up and we headed back home, praying all the way that Daddy would be sobered up or gone. This was just one of many times that I remember us running away in the middle of the night, fearing for our lives. We ran to some old barn, generally in the dead of winter with snow and ice on the ground, and often no hay in the loft to sleep on. That white lightning sure made my Daddy mean.

* * *

Before Christmas, the Lions Club men came to our school and they picked out a certain number of real poor kids from each class and took them to town to the Belk Store. They bought coats, shoes, socks, underpants, and some other things for each child; if you had shoes or a coat already, they bought you other things like pants for the boys or things the girls needed, dresses and such.

They came into my room and the teacher said, "That Long girl over there needs to go."

She took me by the arm and led me to the front of the classroom. All the kids looked at me. Some whispered to each other. Some snickered to each other. I was so embarrassed, I wanted to die.

Mary Judith Messer

The man took me out of the room and told me to stand in the hallway with some other poor kids. Then out came Joe and Cheryl from their rooms.

The man, and two more men, put us in some nice cars and took us to town to the only department store on Main Street. I loved all the nice coats, shoes and dresses I saw. Each man took a few of us at a time. The lady that worked in Belk's helped us try on everything to get our right sizes.

I got a nice long coat, some Mary Jane shoes, some panties, one dress and a blue pair of socks. That was only the second coat I had ever owned. The other one I had was found on the playground at school and the teacher could not find who it belonged to so after the end of the school year, she gave it to me.

I was very happy with all my new things but at first I didn't want to wear them to school. I knew all the kids would know where I got them and make fun of me.

Cheryl and Joe got some nice things also. Joanie was not in school yet. I refused for a long time to wear any of my new things to school. After I saw the other kids and Cheryl and Joe wearing their new clothes, I started to wear mine.

That was the first time I ever had a new pair of panties. Mama usually took the pretty-colored, cotton flour sacks we had and made panties for Cheryl and me. Those store bought ones were so fine and silky. I never wanted to waste them and put them on my bottom and get them dirty, but I began to wonder what they would feel like so I put them on. They were so nice and I looked at them in our old cracked mirror; they were great.

Back to the Test Farm &
More Close Calls

Someway, I did not know how, but Daddy got a job on the State Test Farm. His job was to milk all the cows. So, move we did, up that hill. The little shack we moved to was even smaller than the one we just moved from.

It was a small wooden shack by the creek, just in front of the dairy where Daddy would be milking the cows, the same creek Daddy had caught his muskrats in. We were now back on the State Test Farm.

One day, Mama told us our Papaw, her daddy, was coming all the way from Spartanburg, South Carolina to visit. We knew about our Papaw, but did not remember meeting him before. Mama had two brothers plus her Daddy.

I never met any of Daddy's people, so I didn't know anyone on his side of my family since all his brothers and sisters were given to different families when his mother died. Papaw, Mama's daddy, was coming on a train, she said. We kids were so excited. We were all going crazy. Mama told us to go outside and watch the hill he was going to be coming down. We ran out and kept watch of that hill for hours. Finally, we saw this tall, slender man with a suit and tie come into sight.

"Mama, Mama, Mama!" we cried. "We see someone! Come and see if this is him."

She ran out the kitchen door and said, "Lord yes! That is your Papaw!" And she took off running. She hugged him over and over and cried, "Daddy, I never thought I would see you again."

She brought him in the shack and gave him a chair. He looked so nice with a suit and tie, dress shoes and all. Mama had made us put on our best clothes after we had washed up in the galvanized tub, but nothing looked better than my Papaw. He took a pack of Juicy Fruit gum from out of his vest pocket and gave all four of us a nice stick of gum. He told us how Uncle Zolie was and wanted to know if we had seen Uncle Paul, who lived in Waynesville. He told us all about Spartanburg.

Mama told him Uncle Paul went into the army. He sat me on his lap and talked to me real sweet. I had never had any one I loved to hug me or let me sit on their lap and it was just great. He looked at my fingernails and said, "What is this red stuff on your nails?"

I told him Cheryl had put it on me and it was fingernail polish.

He looked me in the face and said, "God never made you with that red stuff on your nails. Get that off and never put that stuff on again or I will never come back."

I ran crying into the kitchen to find a knife. I got a knife out of a drawer and tried to scrap the polish off. I got most of it off.

Papaw didn't stay long. He had a room in town. We saw him one more time before he went back to South Carolina. We knew when he left we might not ever see him again.

* * *

One wash day, Mama had us carry water and fill up her big iron wash pot on the fire we had built outside. She got the water boiling hot and set two old chairs over and set her galvanized tub on them. Then she carried buckets full of hot water and poured it into her tub.

Cheryl and I went around the house gathering up all the clothing we could find for her to wash. She was going out the door for another bucket of hot water when Joe let out a scream. He had pulled over the tub of hot water.

Moonshiner's Daughter

Cheryl ran outside and grabbed him up and pulled him away from the fire. She poured cool water over him and still he screamed his head off. We all just knew he would die.

He was so lucky he was just scalded on his shoulder and one leg, but from then on, Mama never put heated water where it would be so easy for one of her children to turn it over.

* * *

One hot summer day, Mama decided she was going to walk to town and we children all thought we would be going with her so we started off with her. She took Joanie by the hand and we all walked up this hill behind the shack when we came to this old grey concrete silo, the place farmers put cut up stalks of corn to feed the cows in the winter. Mama made us climb up the side ladder of the empty silo and climb down lots of steps to the inside floor. I remember being so afraid. We were deep inside this huge, tall, round thing. Joe and Joanie both cried for a long time. Mama told Cheryl to look after us and not let us climb out till she came for us. It was so scary inside that thing. We got so hot and tired as we waited for Mama to come fetch us; finally, Joanie cried herself to sleep. At almost dark, we had never been so happy to see Mama, when she poked her head over the top of the silo and called for us to climb back out. I think Cheryl had to put Joanie on her back to get her out.

* * *

We were outside playing one morning when we looked over to the hill and saw a man coming down. We knew it wasn't our Papaw for he didn't dress like that. As he got closer, we could make out a man in a uniform. We ran up the hill to meet him.

It was Uncle Paul. He was on a furlough from the Army. I just loved the way he looked in his uniform, he was so handsome. He visited with us a good while then asked me if I would like to walk to town with him and get an ice cream.

I jumped up and down because he picked me to be the one to go with him to town. The thought of my handsome uncle taking me

Mary Judith Messer

to town and on top of that, an ice cream cone at Smith's Drug Store? I was the happiest kid in the whole wide world.

Uncle Paul said, "Now, now don't get too excited. You will have to go ask your Mom first."

I ran around behind the back of the shack where she was hanging out clothes on the clothesline. "Mama," I shouted. "Can I please, please, go to town with Uncle Paul? He asked me if I wanted to go. Please Mama! Please! He said we will go buy a ice cream cone at Smith's Drug Store. Please, Mama!"

"Okay, okay. Stop making such a big deal out of it. You know the other kids will want to go also. Don't get them all to crying to go, too."

I was so happy I went skipping all around the yard. Then Uncle Paul and I started off. How I just loved him in his nice Army outfit. I just loved the cap, how he wore it on his head. I was so proud to be with him.

We took off up the hill towards Waynesville. We had walked over the little hill and started down the back through the cow pasture when we ran into a man. He stopped to talk to Uncle Paul, they said a few words and Uncle Paul said to me, "Judith, I need to take you back home because me and Bob need to go somewhere."

My heart dropped. I could not say a word. I just turned around and followed him back down the hill to the shack.

Uncle Paul said, "Don't worry, Judith. I will take you for sure soon."

I walked to the long milk barn where Daddy worked, empty by now, across from the shack. I could hardly see for my tears. I found a little corner where no one could see or hear me and I cried for a very long time. After that day, I never loved Uncle Paul. When he came around I would go out of the shack or away from him. I never forgave him. When he got out of the Army, he was a drunk and slept around in old cars and he would even drink paint thinner called Solox or pure alcohol or anything he could buy real cheap, twenty-five cents a bottle. He was in jail for public drunkenness so many times and finally someone found him dead in an old car. He died after my Papaw.

Moonshiner's Daughter

* * *

Every August, the rich people at the State Test Farm had a watermelon party and invited all of us to go. They put up a big tent with long tables and loads of sawdust for the floor. We kids could not wait to go. Friday night we could hardly go to sleep waiting for Saturday to come and the thought of eating all the watermelon we wanted. The next morning, we jumped out of bed, threw on our clothes and raced up the hill to the big tent. It was only 7 am and of course the tables were empty. The party wasn't supposed to start till noon but we couldn't wait. We ran around the tables playing in the sawdust till we got bored. We walked down to the dairy barn to watch Daddy milk as he put those long funny looking things on the cows' bags. He put us to work carrying out the long things with milk in them. After we helped him herd the cows out of the milking barn, we ran over to the shack. We played around the old dirt yard trying to pass the time. Mama made some of her huge biscuits and a pan of gravy and she called us to come eat some. We went in and had a bite to eat but all four of us kept running to the door to see if the watermelon trucks had come up the hill. Finally we spotted three truck filled to the very top of each bed with great big green watermelons.

We started to run up the hill but Mama said, "Don't go so fast, give them time to cut them up and put them out on the tables."

Some cars and trucks were already all lined up the gravel road in front of our shack.

"Mama, can we go now? Please, please, can we? Can we?"

"Okay, okay, but stay out of the road. Walk in the grass. Watch Joanie and Joe. I will come up later."

We four ran all the way to the tent and were out of breath. More cars and trucks were coming and we could see all that watermelon. A man at one table saw the four of us standing at the end of the long tent and told us to come on over to the table.

We went to the table and he gave us all a big piece of the watermelon. I think the man was Mr. W. M. Whisenunt that lived in

Mary Judith Messer

the big white house across the road that has pavement. We started in eating that good, cold watermelon and didn't quit till we thought we would pop. Lord, that was so good and it was in the hot summer. Once every year they had a watermelon party. When we had to move away, I sure missed it.

One day Mama was making blackberry jelly. We had all picked her some berries so she could make us some jelly. She had a big pot on the wood stove. You could see the bubbles and steam. I was standing next to the wood stove and Joe was playing around with this mop. Mama was in the yard washing up some jelly jars in her pot outside. Joe let the mop drop and it landed in the middle of the pot of boiling jelly. I reached to grab it to get it out before Mama came in and gave Joe a beating. When I pulled the mop out of the pot of hot jelly, it came down on my hand and arm. I screamed. My hand and arm were on fire. Joe ran out of the house and Mama never knew he was the one that dropped the mop in the jelly. She was so mad at me that she knocked me out of the door, never mind that I had hot jelly all over my hand and right arm. I have the scars to this day from that burn. Mama never would believe her boy did anything bad.

We got all kinds of beatings on account of Joe. We teased him and he went crying to her. Then we got beat. Anything bad he did, she said that we did it. She told us one day that he was a Price not a Long. His Daddy was a Price. Who knows? We did love him very much as a brother when he wasn't getting us beat up.

One day Mama put this ring on to wear to town. She always put Cheryl to watch us for we never ever wanted to go back to that silo. When she got back from town, she was all upset because her finger was so swollen she couldn't get the ring off. God, she was so scared her finger would have to be cut off. She had all us children running around crying, not knowing what to do or what was going to happen. Her finger was so swollen you could hardly see the ring. Nearly hysterical, I ran out into the road to flag down a vehicle to get help and this man in a black truck threw on his brakes, skidded to a stop, and leaned out his window.

"Why in the hell are you running into the road like that?"

Moonshiner's Daughter

I said, "Mama is going to die if her finger gets cut off."

"What are you talking about?"

I tried to explain what was going on and he finally understood. The man's name was Jimmy Cagle. He got out of his truck, went around the back to his tool box and got out this small saw. When he came in with that saw, Joanie and Joe let out screaming. They thought he was going to cut off Mama's finger.

Mama often told us she was dying or would threaten to kill herself. She would put red mercurochrome on her lips so we would think she had drunk it and then show us the skull and crossbones on the bottle; we knew that meant poison. So Joanie and Joe for sure knew she would die with her finger cut off.

Mr. Cagle held the saw as he pulled back the skin on Mama's finger while we four kids were huddled around crying. He took short strokes till he got the ring cut in two.

When we saw the ring slip off after he put lard on her finger, we all stopped crying and hugged Mama. We were so happy not to lose our Mama. One more time the grim reaper got fooled.

Daddy was always gone when we needed him.

Mary Judith Messer

Finally, A New House &
A New Friend

Daddy must have been doing a good job for the State Test Farm because they decided to build us a new house, a real honest to goodness house. Daddy had quit making moonshine and he was working hard on the farm. Anything around the farm, he was put to help out. He was a very good worker. He worked hard, but he still drank most of the time, even there at the State Test Farm. Living there, he didn't have to pay rent like he did at all the other sharecropper shacks we had lived in and he didn't have to give up half of any crops he made, either. All us kids jumped up and down when we found out we were going to move one day to a brand new house.

Some months after we got that great news, we started back at East Waynesville School. Our school bus stop was right next to the road that went straight through the State Test Farm property. After the bus stopped to let us out, we stepped down and out through the open bus door onto the gravel road. Some of the children called out, "Let's go home to our shack" and the bus full of children all laughed.

I just dropped my head because they could see our little shack from the bus. It was just a hop on the right. We were always being made fun of for our clothing, and we had no shoes. Because of where we lived and everything else, they called us "The Longs, white trash!" Those words hurt almost more than being beaten did.

I had no idea what our Daddy did with his money. I guess he bought whisky because he wasn't making it anymore. When it came time for all the sugar and yeast, he had plenty of money to buy it. Good thing we all got free lunches at school or I guess we would have gone hungry a lot more than we did. We were also made fun of when we got our free lunches.

I walked around school with my head down most of the time. I never looked anyone in the face. I think Cheryl and Joe were just as ashamed as I was. Poor people had a bad life in Haywood County after World War II, and probably most anywhere else, too.

One Saturday, we were out playing in the dirt yard; we saw two large trucks on the paved road. They were loaded with big cinderblocks. We watched them with great curiosity. They backed those big trucks just off the road above the Whisenhunt house. We all ran in the shack and started yelling about the trucks and loads of blocks. Mama was putting a bowl of potatoes on the table. She looked out and told us, sure enough, the blocks were for our house.

A few days after the trucks came, as we were getting off the bus, some boy called out, "Let's all go to our shack."

Cheryl stopped dead. She turned around and said, "You see those things behind that house, behind that white house?"

All the snickering stopped.

"That is going to be our big new house!"

Everyone on the school bus jumped up to look out the left side of the bus to take a look at the blocks for our house.

We could see from our shack the work that was going on at our house. We were not allowed to go to the highway, but one day, we begged so pitifully that Mama let us go part way so we could get a better look.

"Stay in that wheat field on this side of the highway," she told us. "You go into the highway for any other reason and you get your Daddy's belt!"

We knew better than not to mind, when Daddy's belt was mentioned. We were deathly afraid of him. When we had a whipping coming, we all wanted Mama not Daddy to do it, if we just had to be whipped.

We four ran down the little gravel road, then we jumped off to the right into the wheat field. The wheat was just up to my waist and we all got as close as we dared to the highway to get a real good look. We were so excited. We just watched and watched for the

Mary Judith Messer

longest time. The men were digging at something in the ground. There were four men and they were all over the place. We noticed it was getting late.

Then Mama called out, "Cheryl, Judith! Get yourself here!"

We all ran like the wind for we knew we had stayed a bit too long. Mama was mad, but not mad enough for a spanking. She knew how excited all of us were. I think she was pretty excited herself about the new house. She just never let on. Mama's friend, Lucie Ann, came to see her one day. They were talking in the little kitchen. Lucie Ann wanted Mama to go some place with her.

Mama said, "It's a way out of town, Lucie. Terry will not let me go. Will you go over to the dairy and ask him, Lucie Ann?"

Lucie Ann went over the little road in a flash and disappeared inside the milk dairy. She had just gotten out of sight and then, boom, she was back. "Emily, I never got to ask him. He said, "Hell no!" before I could get it all out. He was so mad, he threw a pitch fork at me and only missed my leg by inches."

Lucie Ann never came back much after that, but Mama liked her anyway.

Every day at the bus stop, all the children looked at our house to see just how much work on it had been done. As for us children, we couldn't wait to get off the bus so we could get a real good look. After a few months, a man knocked on our door. Of course, us kids ran all at once to open the door for it was very seldom that anyone came knocking on our shack. It was a man and he called Daddy to the door.

We listened to him and he told Daddy that tomorrow, we would be able to move into our new house. We kids were all running around like the wild bunch, and Daddy called us down. We all knew what that meant, if we didn't quiet down and fast.

Next morning, we went over to the new house. We had one truckload of things to move. So in less than three hours, we were out of the old shack for good.

The new house was bright and smelled good from the fresh lumber and what was really nice--it had this small basement. We rushed from room to room looking it over. It was a pretty wooden

Moonshiner's Daughter

house built on top of cinderblocks. It had two bedrooms, a kitchen, a small porch and guess what, an inside toilet, like at school. It had real electric lights, the first house where we lived that had electricity. Boy, were we set! We kids were on top of the world, we were so excited. And Lord, Mama almost told Daddy to take his belt to us that she had hung beside the wood stove.

The next morning, we came out of our new house to get on the bus; we were all smiles as the kids on the bus watched us. For the first time, I held my head up and looked at them.

* * *

But it was not any better at school. I was in a new grade, but the teacher and the children were still so mean. The kids called me names and one boy stuck a lead pencil in my leg. The lead broke off his pencil and is in my leg to this day.

One day, the teacher told us all to put our hands and our heads on our desks because Mrs. Smith, the school nurse, was coming in to check all our heads for lice and our fingers for itch. Yes, the same Mrs. Smith, the Haywood County Nurse that gave the shots at school,

We all did as told and Mrs. Smith went all over the class with her rubber gloves, looking at heads and fingers.

When she got to me, she said, "So, we have THIS LITTLE CRY BABY, LONG! HA, HA!" and went on.

Every day the teacher said mean things. Joe's teacher beat him with a leather strap two times in one day. We were always getting beat for one reason or another.

One day, we were all in line going out to the playground. I saw that old man that took me to that dark basement. He had a nickel in his hand. I turned my head real fast. I did not want to look at him.

I stayed in line and got close to this girl. I stepped on her heels. She turned around and looked at me, but never said anything. It was Alice Jane Sisk and she was a little friendly with me. We talked on the playground. I did not have friends much and I didn't want to

Mary Judith Messer

make Alice Jane mad. It was pretty cold out and I just had my cotton dress on. Alice Jane was talking with me as we were walking around the schoolyard.

She asked, "Why don't you have a coat? Why doesn't your Daddy buy you one?"

I told her, "We don't have the money. The Lions Club coat got too small. I wore it till my arms were way longer than the sleeves. Now, Joanie has it."

Alice Jane stopped walking, took off her coat and I could see she had a sweater on underneath, and she said, "Here. You can wear my coat till we get back in the classroom." She said she had another coat at home the Lions Club gave her also.

I said, "Thanks," and put it on. It was a warm blue coat with a black fuzzy collar. I remember scrunching up my shoulders toward my ears so I could feel that soft collar around my face. That one little gesture would come back to haunt me later.

Sometimes, another girl in class talked to me also. She was very pretty. She had real long blond hair and wore nice clothes.

I wondered why she was so friendly to me as pretty and nice as she was. Her name was Sandy James. One day she asked me, of all people, "Can you come spend Tuesday night with me?"

I told her, "I'll ask my Mama."

That day after school, I could hardly wait to get home and ask Mama if I could spend the night with Sandy.

Mama didn't want me to go, but with my pleading and begging, she finally gave in, but she said, "It will have to be on a Saturday when you go and spend the night."

The next day I couldn't wait to tell Sandy at school that Mama said I could stay Saturday night. That day Sandy was even friendlier to me out on the playground. I thought, *finally after all these years, I have a true friend.* She even bought me a Brown Mule for recess. We walked and talked all around the playground. In class, she asked our teacher if she could change her desk. She never told the teacher it was so she could sit by me. The boy that put the pencil lead in my leg was happy to move, so he changed his desk gladly. Sandy and I whispered to each other all day; every time the teacher

Moonshiner's Daughter

had her back turned, we were whispering about something and snickering. It was a very happy day for me. It was only Tuesday and Sandy and I could not wait for our sleep over. I still liked Alice Jane, but I just really took up with Sandy. I just could not believe my good luck that Sandy was my friend. I had thought I was just white trash like the kids had called me. *But that couldn't be true,* I thought now, *or how could a girl like Sandy want to play and be friends with the likes of me?* I had to pinch myself to believe it was all real.

Every day for the rest of the week, Sandy and I held hands on the playground. She bought me a cookie or ice cream every day for recess. Finally Friday came, and I said good bye to Sandy as I got on my school bus. We had made plans for me to walk to her house on Saturday. She lived on East Marshall Street. The State Test Farm where I lived was not too far from her house, maybe a twenty-five minute walk.

It was around 11 o'clock when Mama finally let me leave. I went skipping down the highway then I cut down the dirt road in front of the old shack. I walked a little ways and cut up this hill behind the shack. I walked up the hill, climbed though this barb wire fence into the cow pastures, then onto a highway. I walked up the steep roadway past the Haywood County Hospital on down the street, making sure to stay on the sidewalks down the long street past lots of streets. When finally I saw East Marshall Street, I was almost running and could not wait to get to Sandy's house. She was waiting outside and waved to me.

"Judith! Judith! Over here!"

I saw her and ran over to where she was standing. She had such a pretty house, nice flowers and lots of green grass. She took me inside to meet her mom, who was just as pretty as Sandy. Her kitchen was so nice and clean; you could eat off the floor.

"Hi," her mom said to me. Then she talked a little with me and then told Sandy, "Why don't you take Judith out and show her your play house? I will send out some cookies and milk."

Sandy and I went skipping out to her play house. When she opened the door, I almost fell over. She had so many baby dolls, you couldn't even count them. She had some of them at this little doll

Mary Judith Messer

table. They were having tea. Some were in a little kitchen fixing food. Some were in little doll beds, while others were cleaning with brooms and toy mops. A whole family of dolls was playing games. It was a doll family world. How happy Sandy must have been to have such a wonderland of dolls, toys and a big doll house of her own.

She had one brother, but he never came in her play house. She just had all her dolls to play with. What fun!

We sat down in the little chairs. I was very little for my age and I could fit just fine. We played only a short time when she heard her mother call.

She said, "I'll be back in a minute," and ran to her house.

I played with a big pretty doll she called, "Ann." I thought her mother must have called her in to get the cookies and milk. When she came back, though, she had no cookies or milk.

"Judith, Mama asked me to ask you before you can sleep with me tonight, do you have lice?"

"No," I said. "You remember last month when Nurse Smith looked at our heads? She would have told our teacher to get me out of school if I had the lice."

"I believe you, but Mama wants to make sure. You know, if I was to get lice in my long hair, I would just die. Mama said she would have to cut off all my long, blond hair and I would just die. She wants to know if it's okay for her to look in your hair."

I said, "Fine, I do not care. I know I don't have them lice."

Sandy ran to get her mother.

Mrs. James came into the play house and asked, "Is it alright to look at your head, Judith?"

"Sure. I have never had any lice."

She smiled at me and I bent my head down as she gently put her hands in my hair. In just moments, after looking at my scalp, her smile disappeared. "Judith, you do have lice! I am sorry, but you must go home now. Sandy, you go into the house, at once."

Without even a good bye, my first and only best friend Sandy turned and was gone.

Moonshiner's Daughter

I walked out of Sandy's play house, across the lawn of her pretty home and tears started pouring down my face. I think that was the first time my little girl's heart had ever been broken. I was crying so much as I stumbled my way up the street I did not see a truck coming that missed me by only inches. The driver blew his horn several times, but I didn't pay any attention. I cried all the way home.

Mama was real surprised to see me back home. She got so upset when she found out why I was home early and looked at my head. She said, "Who the hell have you been playing with that you caught damn lice from?"

I told her, "Only Alice Jane and Sandy."

She looked at the rest of the kids; no one had lice but me. That was a miracle by itself because Cheryl and Joanie both slept with me in our bed.

She got me down and when she got finished with me, I never had a hair left. She even took Daddy's straight razor and shaved my head. I would not go back to school even if she killed me but she didn't make me go. I was out of school, letting my hair grow out, for over a month. Finally she made me go back even though my hair was still very short.

As soon as I got on the bus that first morning with my short hair after being out for so long, everyone began making fun of me and Joe started in fighting with one kid after another. I started fighting, too, and so did Cheryl. We busted a nose or two. I got a cut lip and Joe a bloody nose. One thing about us Longs, when one of us got into trouble, we all got into the fight. We took up for each other, but we also fought each other like cats and dogs. At home, we older kids were always getting whipped for teasing Joe. That made us want to tease him more, and then he would go tattling on us, running to Mama.

At school, Sandy had the teacher move her back to her old desk, as far away from me as she could get. The teacher liked her a lot, so she moved her without a word. Sandy didn't ever speak one word to me again. I think Sandy thought that if she talked to me, I

Mary Judith Messer

would give her lice. Well, if it was that easy to get lice, we'd all have them, wouldn't we?

Nurse Smith came back to school three days after I was back, and she went to all the classrooms to look for lice and itch. She started to look at my head, but stopped short.

"So, Long," she said, "you had them lice and now you don't!" The whole classroom broke out in laughter. She could see all over my head without even touching my head.

Alice Jane came up to me after my long absence from school and she asked me, "Why have you been out of school for such a long time?"

I thought, *Is she crazy or something? Doesn't she see my hair?* She didn't say a single word about my hair. I just stood there staring at her when something popped into my mind. I thought, *"You, hussy! You're the one who gave me the lice that day I put on your coat."* I just stood in the school hallway looking at her, but revenge grabbed my heart.

After we got off the bus that evening, Joe said, "Hey, Sis, you know what? I told that nurse she didn't have to look at my hair. I didn't have no big lice. I only had small ones!"

We all laughed at him. I told him, "You better hope that you don't have a one."

Sweet Revenge &
A Ruined Christmas Play

One of our favorite places to play was on this hill out from the house on this huge cement thing. It had four corners and one hole in the top. I think it used to be somebody's water reservoir. We all liked to swing down in it. One day at school, I told Alice Jane, "You should stop by and see our new house and play some with Cheryl and me."

She said, "Sure, if it is not too far from where I live."

She lived at the foot of Hall Top Road, in Waynesville, so one day at school, she said, "I will come and see you on Saturday. My mother told my dad to run me over, but I will have to walk back home."

I said, "Fine."

That Saturday morning, Alice Jane got there around 11:30. Joe, Cheryl and I went and showed her all around the house. She liked the house for it was better than her house. Her house was by this old gravel road and when cars passed fast, they threw dust and rocks into her little plank house. Our house was up above the highway so we never got any dust off the road.

We took Alice Jane out to our favorite playhouse, the big gray cement reservoir. She thought it was real cool. We played a little and this wise idea popped in my mind. I knew I didn't like that girl. Every time I looked at her, I saw lice and felt shame.

Mama called out for Cheryl to come help her, so she went to the house. Alice Jane and I climbed down into the reservoir through the hole in the top. Inside, there was all kind of trash, some old newspapers and paper boxes and other stuff.

I climbed out with Joe's help and told Alice Jane I had to run to use the bathroom and I would be right back. I ran to the house and found where Mama kept her long box of kitchen matches and shoved a few of them into my pocket. I will never know just what was really on my mind! Then I ran back to the old cement reservoir and climbed up on it.

Alice Jane was still down on the concrete floor inside the reservoir. She was too small to climb up on her own. She had tried to climb out, but fell back in. Joe was on the top of it just playing around. I got on top and went over to the open hole then took a long match out of my pocket. I struck it on the cement top, it caught fire and I dropped the flaming match down the open hatch. It landed in the old newspapers and set fire to them right away.

As soon as I saw the fire start, I got Joe to help me push the big heavy lid over the hole. We heard Alice Jane start to scream and cough. We watched as the smoke began to pour out of the cracks on the top. Alice Jane cried and screamed even louder.

I then got Joe to help me with the lid and we slide it back from the hole.

Joe and I peered down into the fire pit and we could see that Alice Jane was almost black from the smoke. I reached down and pulled her out with Joe helping me. She had peed and messed on herself.

I said, "I don't think you will ever give me the lice anymore, will you?" She was still crying and snot was all over her face. She ran home and we watched her go out of sight. Later on, I thought a lot about that trick I pulled. I never meant to kill her, but, boy, I was mad enough to kill her. My hair still was very short.

* * *

We kids sure liked our new house. We never had much furniture in it. In Cheryl, Joanie's and my room, we only had a bed and a closet. In Mama and Daddy's room, they had a bed and an old dresser Mama had before they were married. Joe slept on the couch which was the only thing in the living room except the wood heater.

Moonshiner's Daughter

In our kitchen, we had a wooden table someone had made for us, a few chairs, a wood cook stove and a white dish cabinet that also had a place for flour and meal.

Christmas was coming and it would be the first Christmas in our new house. We never got a Christmas tree or anything like that. Mama always tried to crack out her black walnuts to sell so she could get us some nuts and stick candy, an orange or two. The week before this Christmas, a lady from the local Baptist Church paid us a visit. The children in the church were putting on a Christmas Story about Jesus being born. The lady asked Cheryl and me if we would come and be in the play. She said we all could have a bag of nuts, an orange and candy if we would come. It was not too far to the church. The road was paved and we could walk to it in less than half an hour.

Mama said it was okay for us to be in the play.

The lady made us promise to be at the church on Wednesday night to practice the play.

Cheryl and I walked to the church on Wednesday night. It was dusty and already dark when we got there. We spent two hours learning our parts. Then the lady gave us all our parts on paper to take home to study.

Cheryl and I were pretty scared when we started walking home. We stayed close together and ran most of the way. When I got home, I could not find my part in the play nowhere. I had put it in my pocket but had lost it. Sunday was the play and I didn't know what to do those three days till the play. We had no phone, so we couldn't call the church.

The next morning Mama woke me up real early right after day light. She said, "You and Joe go look for that paper. Watch out for cars because lots of people will be going to work. Try to find it before it gets blown off the road." We walked all the way to the church and back, but never found it. I thought, *what in the world will I do?*

Saturday night a boy from the church came by and said, "You have to come for rehearsal Sunday morning before Sunday school."

Mary Judith Messer

Cheryl had studied her part for three days. I had forgotten my part because it had been read to me only one time. When we got to church Sunday morning, the lady gave me the part again and I was so relieved. We went over the play. I had not studied the part but I knew I was one of the wise men with this white robe on. Cheryl was Mary, Jesus' mother. She knew her part good. I read over my part a hundred times. I was getting real good at it. Cheryl and I walked home from the church, and I said my part over and over till I had it down pat.

Sunday night, play night, finally came and we all went to church. Just us kids of course, because we all wanted to get a bag of nuts, oranges and stick candy they were giving everyone at church for Christmas as a gift.

We all put on our long white sheet robes and got ready for the play. It was such fun to see everyone all dressed up. Each of us was to walk out on the stage in front of the curtain, tell who we were and what part we were going to play, then come back behind the curtain to get the play started.

Cheryl went out to tell everyone who she was. Then, it was my turn. I walked out toward the stage, feeling real brave. The second I got in front of the curtain, I could see lots of people in the audience, everyone looking at me. I opened my mouth to say my words and all I could do was look at all those eyes on me. I could not move. My lips were frozen. I was just like a cold dead statue. I could not even close my mouth, let alone open my teeth to say a word. My mind was all gone. I started to shake. Not one person made a sound in the audience. Then from behind the curtain came the long stick with the curve on it that was made into a shepherd's staff. Someone hooked me by the leg and pulled me back behind the curtain.

Then I came out of the trance I was in. From all the laughter I heard, everyone was just howling out loud. I sat down in a chair behind the curtain, which was a good thing, because I could not look at anyone. I was the most embarrassed and had never felt so ashamed.

All the other children were wonderful in the play but it was short one wise man because of me. Some of the kids in the play rode my bus every day and I knew what kind of mess I would be in Monday on the bus.

Cheryl got two bags of treats, including one for me also. I wouldn't come out from behind the curtain till almost everyone in the church left.

We walked home, Cheryl, Joe and Joanie, all eating the candy and nuts and all. I just held my bag in my hand. I thought *I am just a pitiful mess. I have no brains. I have no sense.* I was so sad. I messed up everything. The lady who put on the play never scolded me or nothing. It was all the laughter that made me want to die.

Sure enough, after Christmas when we did go back to school, on the bus it was bad, real bad. The six kids that had been in the play started before I could even find me a seat. They called me all kinds of very bad names. Behind me someone jerked my hair and spit balls hit me in the face. I was in tears.

Joe was only a little boy, but he punched and fought all he could. Cheryl had a girl by the hair. My nose was pouring blood. Everyone on the bus was fighting us. I had tried to get Mama to not make me go to school but she wouldn't hear of it.

The bus driver stopped two times to call down everyone, but it only stopped till he took off again. We finally got to school and the bus driver wouldn't let anybody get off. The front of my dress was all bloody. Cheryl's hair was all pulled out. Joe also had a bloody nose.

The driver got out of the bus and shut the door behind him. When he came back, he had the principal. We now knew why we were not getting off. He opened the door to the bus after he talked to the principal a short time.

We knew for sure we were in big trouble. The principal made all the kids leave the bus except us three Longs. I thought, *what's going on?* I tried to tell him that the other kids had started the whole thing. I was shaking all over; my feet and legs wouldn't be still. He had the driver go get another teacher. He dragged me out of the bus,

Mary Judith Messer

the driver had Joe and the other teacher had Cheryl. We all screamed and cried and tried to get away.

They drug all three of us into his office. We could see the windows full of children looking at us as we were dragged up the steps to the office. The hallways were full of children looking at us.

The teacher and driver stood guard at the door. We tried to talk to the principal, to tell him we had not started the fight. No one heard. He took out this long leather strip with round holes in it. He had beat Joe with it before. He took Cheryl and said, "You Longs are always into something!" Then he hit Cheryl three hard licks. Cheryl never made a sound. She just closed her eyes. Then the principal snatched Joe and hit him three times, and his nose started to bleed again, but not a sound did he make. He then took me and as he did, I twisted my arm around and he lost his grip on me. Then the other teacher stepped over and grabbed one arm and the principal grabbed the other. They both threw me over the desk. The principal hit me four times. By the second lick, I did not feel the licks. My bottom was numb. The principal then told us to get to the rest room and clean up, and if we ever fought on school grounds or the bus again, we would get twenty-five licks each.

We went to the bathroom and took Joe in with us. We took some paper towels, wet them and washed Joe's face and nose best we could. He had blood on his only pair of overalls. We hoped Mama could wash it out. Cheryl and I washed the best we could with those old stiff paper towels. I tried to get the blood off the front of my dress. I think it was my blood and the other girl's that I had by the hair. Her nose also got smashed.

All day in class the other kids tried to stay away from me. Some even moved out of their own desks and sat in desks that belonged to someone who was out of school that day just to get away from old Judith Long. I guess the blood on my dress made them sick or maybe it was just me. Who knows? I just did not care.

The Red Devil & Mama Nearly Dies

That afternoon on the bus, lots of the kids made fun of us, but we looked out the window. Someone pulled my hair, but I tried not to pay it much attention. We were all glad when the bus finally stopped in front of our house. We ran down the aisle in a hurry to get off, but as I went by, a boy stuck his foot out and I had to catch a seat back before I fell to the floor. We ran up to our house. Mama was sweeping off the back porch. She took one look at our faces and almost fainted.

She was mad as hell, but this time, she never went to school. I think somehow she thought we started the fight, but she had her own troubles. Daddy was drinking a lot more. Some nights, she took us out walking to get away from him.

We sometimes walked along the highway near where a friend of Mama's lived. Her friend couldn't walk. She had had polio when she was young and walked a little with crutches. Her name was Susan Jane Jonas.

We walked to Susan's one night and as we walked, we kids looked up into the sky. We watched the stars; they were so pretty and bright. I wished I could be up there, sitting on a star in the beautiful, big sky. We saw a star fall or what it looked like to us. The night was very dark. We could not see a moon; we saw a plane with its lights flashing which was very unusual since we never saw many planes.

On the way back home from Susan's, we were about half way home when Mama said, "What is that?"

We all looked down and out the road, the way she was looking. It was a good ways past Susan's house, down the highway.

We stopped and kept watching. It looked red and round and looked like it was moving.

Mama grabbed Joanie by the hand and said, "Kids walk fast, real fast."

We looked back and this big round, red thing was getting closer. It looked like a big ball of fire. We took out running and we ran all the way home. We ran into the basement for we thought if Daddy was asleep, we didn't want to wake him and get beat. There was only one window in the door, and we kids were too afraid to peep out. Mama looked out.

We kids got as far back in the basement as we could get and crowded in a little huddle as Mama watched out the window for a long time.

Then, finally she came back with us and sat down beside us on the old dirt floor. We were so afraid; we didn't go out all night, just went to sleep on the dirt. Mama went to sleep, too. No blankets, no nothing, just the old dirt floor. I shook half the night and finally I fell asleep.

The next morning, we heard Daddy walking upstairs. He woke up at 5:30 every morning to go milk the cows. We waited until he was gone and Mama helped us out of the cold basement.

Before we walked outside, we looked all around to make sure that red thing was not around because it was still dark outside. We got in our beds, but just lay wide awake. We never did find out what that thing was.

But one night, it was raining cats and dogs. There was a very loud knock on the door. We were afraid to open the door. Daddy was off in town getting drunk, and Mama just stood there, wringing her hands.

Again, we heard a very loud knock. Mama tried to peep out the window, but she couldn't see on the porch.

Then someone shouted, "Emily, open the door! God! Open the door!"

Mama ran to the door, opened it and in fell Uncle Paul, her brother, who stumbled in all the way to the wood heater. He was muddy as a dog and crying his eyes out. We all knew he was drunk, but he kept talking about the Devil.

Mama tried to talk to him, but she could not make out what he was saying. "The Devil something"…She gave him some buttermilk, hoping it would sober him up. He sat down at the kitchen table and said, "Sis, I am going to die. You know the devil was after me. This huge, red as fire thing with red glowing eyes was after me on the road. The faster I ran, the faster it came." Uncle Paul cried for hours.

Finally Daddy came home. He also was soaking wet and very drunk, but he had not seen the Devil. He and Uncle Paul stayed up most the night, Paul talking about the Devil and Daddy just mumbling.

The next morning, Uncle Paul was sound asleep in the floor by the heater. He got up after Mama called him to get him some gravy and some of those nice biscuits she always made.

He was dirty and sick. He told Mama, "You know, Sis, the Devil almost got me last night." Here he was, all sobered up and still talking about the Devil. We all believed him for we saw it ourselves. Never again would any of us go out in the dark at this place again.

* * *

One day Mama was going to walk to town with Daddy. Mama left the younger kids in Cheryl's and my care. We were on the porch as we watched them climb the hill behind the shack and go out of sight. She left us a lot when she went somewhere, so we knew how to watch out for the younger ones.

They had been gone for around a half hour when we saw Mama coming back down the hill. She was walking pretty fast. When she got up the steps of the house, we could all see she was crying. She walked past us without a word, went into the bathroom and got something.

We couldn't see what she got so we followed her out of the house, and back down the steps, heading for the basement. By this time we were running after her. She was crying very hard. We kept

Mary Judith Messer

running after her. She rushed down into the basement and locked the door behind her.

Each of us tried to look in the basement window at one time. We bigger ones pushed the little ones out of the way. We watched Mama put this red bottle to her lips. We knew now that it was that poison she always showed us with the skull and cross bones on it. By now we were all screaming. We saw her face. There was red on her lips and she didn't wear lipstick.

We beat on the door, crying and screaming. We all knew our Mama was going to die.

This went on for the longest time, and then Cheryl and I saw her pick up this old rope that was lying in the basement. She tied it into a loop and then wrapped it around her neck. She got up on this rusty bucket and stood on top. She put the rope around one of the rafters and tried to tie it up there. But when the bucket turned over and she fell to the dirt, the rope fell also. We kept screaming as we beat on the door. We hit it so hard; blood poured out of Cheryl's hands and fists and my hands were bloody also. *If only the Whisenhunt's were home, they could come help us.* They both worked and they had their little kids with babysitters.

Mama got up and climbed back on the bucket. She still had the noose around her neck. The other part of the rope was in her hands. This time, she got the other end tied around the rafter. Cheryl and I watched when the bucket turned over again and she fell hanging by her neck. Cheryl grabbed a rock and crashed it into the window. She stuck her hand through the broken glass and got hold of the lock and turned it. We burst through the door and grabbed Mama's legs; boy, she was very heavy. Even Joe helped hold her up by the legs. Cheryl stood on the bucket and somehow she got the rope loose. Joe and I both were very small. It was a miracle that we held her up until Cheryl could get her untied. She plopped to the ground with a thump.

We all knew she was dead. We rubbed her face, hands and arms, and then we got a bucket of water from upstairs. It was a good thing we had running water in this house. This was the first time we ever had water in our house. If we would have had to run to a spring to get water, Mama would have died. We took the full bucket of water and poured it on her head and she came to with a start.

Thinking back, I believe that Mama wasn't able to hang herself because God did not want four little kids to be left with a father like we had. Just what would have become of us kids? Mama was always saying she was drinking that poison red stuff. We would beg her, when we saw the red stuff on her lips, "Please Mama, please don't die! Please Mama, please."

Mama never told us why she had come back that day from town and tried to kill herself. I think she and Daddy had a fight or something. Maybe she saw a woman he had been with. *No matter what, living with the constant threat of your mother wanting to kill herself was something that marked us kids for our whole lives.*

Mary Judith Messer

Santa Visits & We Move To Hell

Our second Christmas in this new house was coming up. It was the day before Christmas. We kids all knew Mama had sold her black walnuts. We had candy, oranges and nuts on our minds. All day we tried to find where Mama had hidden the goodies.

Mama made these huge cakes of corn bread that would just melt in our mouths. We had just eaten our supper of the corn bread and beans, and Cheryl and I were washing up the dishes when this knock came on our door.

Joe ran and opened it, and who was standing there, but old Santa. We all had learned about this fellow a lot but had never seen him in person. Now here he was standing at our door. Of all people, Santa at our door, the Long's door!

He said, "HO, HO, HO!" Joanie was real scared, but Cheryl, Joe and I weren't afraid.

He stepped into the room with this big bag on his shoulder. He opened it and out came a big toy truck for Joe. Next he took out this box with a big doll for Joanie. She didn't want to come get it. She had big eyes and fingers in her mouth and just stared.

I took it and gave it to her. It was almost as big as she was. She hugged it to her heart. Next, he pulled out a bigger box. It was full of oranges and nuts. He then pulled out a box with a doll for me, and one for Cheryl. I saw Cheryl's doll through the front of the box. It was a lot prettier than mine, but I loved my baby just as well.

Mr. Santa went back out on the porch and came back with two huge boxes of food: canned food, sugar, flour, meal, beans, and all kinds of things. You name it, we had it. We could not believe that Santa also brought food as well as toys for good little kids. We must have all been very good to get all those toys for Christmas. Daddy was gone and he never got to see Santa. Santa left us with all our nice toys and food.

We opened the boxes. How nice the baby dolls were! Cheryl opened her box and one of the prettiest dolls in the whole wide world came out. Cheryl held it to her heart and said, "Judith, this is Patsy." We played till Mama made us finish the dishes. Then she made us go to bed.

We all were up Christmas morning at daylight, Joe first to play with his big red truck, then we heard him in the living room and then all of us got up.

We played all day long with our dolls until Mama called Cheryl to come and peel some potatoes. She was fixing a Christmas supper. She had saved up money and bought a fat hen from the farm. This year she just had one cake. It was a big, chocolate one she got uptown. She made that good chicken and dumplings like when we were living in Ninevah. She made the very best chicken and dumplings that day with her big biscuits. I can taste it now. We never ate big meals much during the rest of the year, but we were blessed on account of our Mama on Christmas. Daddy was drunk, but not mean drunk.

We were out of school for a week for Christmas. When we returned to school, I had on a new coat and some shoes. The Lions Club took us again, us poor Longs, and got us some new things or we would not have anything to wear. I tried my best not to drink any water at school. I never wanted to have to go to the rest room before recess. I was afraid I would run into that dirty old man from the basement. Every day as we went to the lunch room, or outside at recess, I saw him always standing with his long handle push broom and I saw his nickel. Two times, I saw a girl go down the steps in front of him. It was the same little girl both times. I think I saw her in the first grade as I passed her room.

Joe was always getting spanked in the principal's office. He was always beat up. Cheryl and I tried to keep out of trouble. If someone pulled our hair, or stuck us with a pin on the bus, we tried not to fight, but we could just take so much, then we would fight.

Mary Judith Messer

One night we got a knock on the door. We thought it was Uncle Paul, but what a big surprise. It was Uncle Zolie, Mama's older brother, all the way from Spartanburg, South Carolina.

We had never seen him but one time before, and he was so good looking, a big man, not short like Uncle Paul, and Mama was very happy to see him. She asked him all about his wife, about our Papaw and all. They talked all night long. He stayed two days with us and I never saw him again. He was very nice to us kids and played with us some. I will always remember Uncle Zolie. We found out a year after he came to see us, he had died. I don't know why Mama never went to the funeral, if they had one. Zolie told Mama that our Papaw sent her his love. He was still living in Spartanburg.

Daddy was still drinking all the time. He went to town and came back very drunk on the days he set his traps and on other days, he worked on the farm. We just hated to see him come home. We could tell by the way he walked if he was mean drunk or just drunk, drunk. He came home one night and told us he was going to buy some land and a house up in the mountains in a place called Foggy Creek. We did not know at all where he got money to buy land and a house. Not even Mama knew. All we knew was we were leaving the State Test Farm after we have lived in three different places on it.

The first place I recall was the Lester Teater Place. The second place was the little shack and then, the third place was the new house they built just for us.

I was glad to leave East Waynesville school, but not glad to leave our house. If I knew then what was to happen in our lives in Foggy Creek, where we were headed, I would have run away, but you never know the future so I took it the best I could, being only nine years old.

Daddy borrowed a truck from someone on the Farm for the move. Later on in years, I learned who the Santa was. It was our next door neighbor, Mr. Whisenhunt, who had been so wonderful to a bunch of poor kids. We were all very sad to leave our home, all except Daddy. We learned later that he was fired at the Farm for his drinking and for beating on Mama.

Moonshiner's Daughter

The move took two truck loads. Cheryl and I were with the first load. Daddy drove the truck deeper, deeper into the mountains. We had long passed the end of the highway and the old mountain road just kept winding. I was getting sicker and sicker by the minute. My head was pure spinning.

I told Daddy, "I need to vomit!" He pulled over a little to get out of the road. The road was so narrow, if another car came, it couldn't pass. As soon as the door opened, I vomited. I was so, so sick.

Cheryl said, "Your face is as white as a sheet."

Daddy said, "Are you done? Get back in here. We got to get going. I have another load before dark."

We drove deeper into the mountains and the road was almost no road at all. We drove right through a creek, no bridge at all, then another creek. By now the road was only about a horse and buggy road. Bushes hit the sides of the truck. We came to a field on the right.

Daddy said, "That is my piece of land that we passed."

There's only one very small shack on the right and I asked Daddy, "Does anyone live in that shack?"

"Of course," he said. "A real old woman and her girl."

We went on up the ditch of a road and he pointed out up to the left where the Franks live, Jim Frank. Just around the turn on the right side of the road was an old log barn. We drove a little more and saw this rundown shack with an old rock chimney.

Daddy stopped right next to the old porch and got out. "Girls, you are home," he said.

All Cheryl and I could do was look at each other. A big pine tree stood in the yard. High weeds were everywhere.

Daddy said, "Now what are you sitting in there for? Get out, but watch every step you take. This is snake country, rattlers and copperheads!"

Now for sure Cheryl and I didn't want to get out. We finally eased out. The first thing Daddy pulled out of the truck was a broom and he handed it to Cheryl, "Here, go clean the house up before I put

Mary Judith Messer

this stuff in. That's the reason why I brought you two in the first load. Judith, get in there and help her."

The front porch steps shook as we walked up to the door. We peeped in to make sure there weren't any snakes in the shack before we stepped inside. It wasn't too bad. It had a kitchen, small living room with a rock fire place and two very small bedrooms in the back. You walked into the kitchen and opened the old door and walked onto a small porch. Then you could walk into the bedrooms from there; the place was full of trash and we swept and swept for a long time.

Daddy rushed us to hurry up and finish. He wanted to get the stuff in and go back after another load.

We got it as clean as we could. He then put Cheryl and me to helping unload. He set up our bed in the back bedroom and said, "All you kids sleep in here." He put his and Mom's bed in the other bedroom and the kitchen table in the kitchen. All the floors were old rough wooden planks-- in some places you could see under the floor to the dirt underneath.

We asked Daddy, "Where is our school?"

"You will all go to Fine's Creek school." All three of us would be in this school when it started in the fall. Joanie was still too young to go to school.

Daddy said, "Stay inside the shack and watch our stuff while I go back for the rest of our things and Joe, Mama and Joanie."

We wondered why he told us to watch the things since we hadn't seen a single soul since we drove into Foggy Creek.

When Daddy got back with Mama, she was just as stunned as we were. We sure had lived in some bad places before, but this one took the cake. As bad as the shack was, it was in the middle of all those woods and weeds were everywhere. We were afraid for days to go outside, but we had to. When we went outside to use the bathroom, we had to use the creek because there wasn't an outhouse. We never had any water inside and no electric lights.

Daddy chopped down a trail on the hill to the spring. He said, "There's nothing like good mountain water right out of the rocks."

Moonshiner's Daughter

I thought, *"Yes, but who has to carry every drop?"* I wanted to say it, but I dared not say a word. Cheryl and I said this to ourselves.

Daddy finally took his old swing blade and cut down the high weeds because Mama was afraid to let us out of her sight.

Daddy said, "Snakes are not the only thing in these mountains. There are plenty of black bears and some panthers too."

Two days after we moved in, Daddy was tramping through the woods looking for a good place with plenty of water to set up his moonshine still. I do not know where he had that old copper still hidden, but he came in with it one day. Old Pat, our horse, pulled a sled with the still on it. Old Pat had been in the pasture with the cows at the State Test Farm.

Mama had to make a trip to town for there wasn't a store until you got into Waynesville. She walked over a mile to the mail boxes and waited until the mailman came, then she rode to Waynesville in his mail wagon. It was an old Jeep wagon. It was at those mail boxes where we were to catch the school bus every morning. *Daddy sure got us back in the sticks.*

At Clyde Ray's Grocery Store, she ran into a friend of Daddy's. If she had not, I do not know how she would have gotten back. She had taken Joe with her and she would not have gotten back until the next day when the mail wagon came back up Foggy Creek if she had not ran into this Welch man to find out he and his wife and real young boy and girl lived way on up in the mountains, almost to the top of Cataloochee.

When Jess Welch drove up with Mama and Joe, Daddy was very friendly. Jess helped Daddy unload his sugar and stuff. As soon as Jess drove off, Daddy walked behind Mama and hit her in the mouth with his fist and to beat it all, he was not even drunk. He beat the very hell out of her and we kids could not do anything, but scream and cry. Her face was black and blue for a month. Her lips were cut. She had bruises on her whole body. She was in worse shape than we had ever seen her. He even kicked her in the ribs and we knew he had broken her ribs because she coughed and spit up blood for a very long time. What in the world could four kids do? He was such a big, tall man. Joe would take his little fists and hit

Mary Judith Messer

him, but it was like hitting a brick wall. He would take his big hands and throw him back to the ground. We were all very afraid of him.

This is the same type of still that Daddy had only his was back in the woods, next to a creek, where no one would find it.

Mountain Living & Finally A Car

Cheryl and I, the two oldest, always had to do all the hard work. The spring was way up above the shack. We hated wash day. We took two big water buckets each and climbed up the hill to the spring. With this long handled dipper, we slowly filled our buckets to the top.

We had to build a fire under Mama's big black pot, and then carry water to fill up her long galvanized tub, so she could have rinse water. It was an all day job which we did almost every Saturday. We never had many clothes (I guess that's why today, I have three big buildings full of clothing.) We would pull off our clothes so she could wash them and would put on a rag waiting for our things to be washed. She took the old wash board, placed it into hot water and put in some kind of suds, if she had some. If not, she used her lye soap to scrub up our clothing. Then we would help her hang them on the clothes line to dry.

At night, before dark, Cheryl and I had to go back up to the spring and get water for the night. We had to cut blocks of wood into stove wood with a sharp ax so she could cook for us. We always had to watch out for Joe and Joanie. We had to carry more water to heat for us kids' baths. I do not remember Daddy ever taking a bath. We kids washed up in Mama's long tub maybe once a month. The hardest of some of the jobs Cheryl and I had to do were the water carrying and wood busting.

I was so skinny and little. Cheryl was not much bigger, but she was taller than me. We got mad sometimes because Joe and Joanie never had to do one thing but play, but we made sure Mama never heard us complain.

Daddy was always in the woods. I think he was guarding his moonshine still. If he was not making the stuff, he was running it off into his jars. He did grow him some tobacco and corn on the piece of land he had shown us the first day I ever laid eyes on Foggy Creek. He put Cheryl and me right in the field working and sometimes Mama would help out.

One day Mama was working with us in the tobacco field and she took her wash tub and put Joanie in it at the top of the field, so she wouldn't get hurt or lost or snake bit. We were all in the middle of the field hoeing when all at once we heard Joanie screaming her head off. We turned around just in time to see her and the tub rolling out of sight down the mountain. We all threw down our hoes and ran after her.

Mama screamed, "Terry! Terry!", but he was all the way on the other side of the field with Old Pat plowing.

We ran down the steep mountain and finally got to Joanie. She was screaming at the top of her lungs, but had only hurt her head a little. She had tried to stand up in the tub and when she did, it started rolling down the mountain. She had held on for dear life, but how she did, we sure didn't know. She went over lots of big rocks. If her head had hit any one of them, I guess she would have been killed. From then on, whenever she was out in the field, Mama took the sash of an old robe of hers and tied Joanie around the waist then tied it to a tree where she could keep an eye on her.

Daddy called Cheryl and me to him a few days after we had moved to Foggy Creek and said, "I am telling you one time and one time only, you are never to get around those Lance boys that live up the Old Road."

This was how we found out that we had another neighbor. The Lances lived a good distance above our spring. We had heard dogs barking and a cow mooing, but we had no idea that someone lived up there. We knew about Jess Welch. His wife was the sister to the Lance man's wife. The Lances had four boys, but I only knew the names of three of them: Jack, Zeb and Lester. I never knew what the other one was called. He was very badly crippled. We found out he crawled around the house with his legs bent double. We later

Moonshiner's Daughter

found out, Lester was the oldest, almost seventeen. Zeb and Jack were almost as big.

We knew Daddy meant what he said when he told us anything and we never went above the spring. Now and then we saw the Lance's black truck go up the Old Road. We tried not to look at it when we were out playing or in the old log barn.

The barn was only a hop from our shack. When we climbed up in the loft, it looked somewhat like the old barn in Ninevah. Down below were stalls just like in Ninevah's barn and a loft. We kids had some good fun in the hay stored there.

Below Daddy's tobacco field, he grew some corn. If he hadn't grown corn, I don't know how we would have eaten. He took it to the old corn mill at the end of Fines Creek and had some ground up into corn meal during the summer. He also used the ground up corn to make moonshine. We didn't starve to death. We ate bread and Mama got some cow's milk from the Jim Frank family on the left about a half mile down the road. She only paid Mrs. Frank twenty five cents for a big jar of sweet milk. Sometimes she let us have butter milk and a big round of homemade butter. I just loved a big hot piece of Mama's corn bread and that butter! You never tasted anything like it.

We were playing in the old barn on the big logs when we saw snakes and we screamed for Mama, but when the snakes saw us, they slid behind the big logs in the barn. We ran and told Mama. She grabbed a hoe and ran with us to chop them up, but they were all out of sight behind the logs. We also saw snakes on the outside of the old rock fireplace. They stuck out their heads. Mama also saw them. She said, "They are copper heads" and she warned us every time we went outside, "Be careful and watch out for snakes!" Daddy killed so many snakes; I lost count when it was up to forty-seven. Those mountains and our yard were just full of them. The barn and rock chimney were also.

We found out from the Frank man that school was starting the next week. Mama got busy washing Joe's only pair of overalls. Cheryl and I had our clean dress. Neither of us had shoes and Joe

Mary Judith Messer

didn't either. Of course, that got us to thinking about how we would get to school in the first place.

"Daddy, where does the school bus stop?" I asked one morning.

"I'll show you" he said and he hitched up Old Pat to the sled.

We wondered *what was he going to haul on the sled?* We found out…It was us! Daddy put Joe, Cheryl and me on the sled then down the Old Road we went. The road was only meant for a sled anyway. It was all washed out and the banks were sliding down in some places. We rode the sled past the tobacco field, on past the Shelley's shack, and then past a barn below the road. It was an old barn that looked like it would fall down. And we kept on a going.

I said, "Daddy, did we pass the bus stop?"

"No." Still onward we went.

Even with Old Pat trotting, it took us a half hour to get to the mail boxes where the bus stop was. Once there, we turned around and headed back for home. Us kids just looked at each other…the mail boxes seemed nearly a mile away. We knew better than to say a word. We were supposed to be at the bus stop at 7:30 every morning. It was the last stop and the furthest stop and when it snowed, the bus didn't even try to make it up there.

Walking that old dirt road was bad that first day of school. Barefooted of course, we stumped our toes on the rocks, leaving a small bloody trail. We were give out when we finally got to the bus stop just barely in time to watch it drive up and start turning around.

Just us older three got on the bus. Mama kept Joanie. She thought she was too young to go to school because she was only four and a half years old. Always before when school started the first day, Mama went to school with us. This time she did not go with us. I think she thought that Cheryl and I could take Joe to his right room by ourselves and get to our own rooms.

Some of the kids on the bus just stared at us, and some were whispering. Also, they were making fun of us on our first day. Some other poor kids like us were on the bus, and they made fun of them, too.

Moonshiner's Daughter

The first day was okay. We all managed to get in the right classes. What we dreaded was the long walk home that evening. After getting off the school bus and the walk home, we had to cut some firewood and carry it inside, put it in big piles in the wood box. Then we had to carry our water down. As we were dipping water, I looked over behind Cheryl and I saw a big fat snake laying right behind her heels. I hollered, "SNAKE!"

Cheryl jumped just as it struck; it missed her leg only by an inch. I lost my balance and fell back. I reached for a big rock and threw it, but missed. It had crawled off fast. Cheryl and I shook all over. We finally got back to the shack with the water after I had fallen two times and spilled my water and had to go back for more. It takes a good long time to fill a bucket with a dipper.

Mama and Daddy just said, "You kids will have to just watch out where you step."

* * *

Joe and I were walking in the woods one day while Daddy was in the tobacco suckering it. (He suckered it by snapping off the little side tobacco leaves so the bigger main leaves would get all the plant's energy and grow bigger.)

We went roaming around in the woods and came up on a big still. We just stopped and looked it over. We knew it wasn't Daddy's because we had already been to his. Lots more people had stills in the woods. We never said anything about it to Daddy. We had been told to stay out of those woods.

We all helped Daddy in his tobacco. We helped work it up and he packed it on long round baskets made of wood. He borrowed a truck from some man he knew, packed the tobacco on the truck and told Mama he would be back soon. He was going to the Asheville Tobacco Warehouse. We watched him drive out of sight.

Mama said, "When he gets back with the money, I will take all you kids to town and get some school clothes."

Mary Judith Messer

It was two weeks before Daddy came home and not one dime did he have. We had no food, but corn bread and milk. The corn ears had all gotten hard and we could not eat it. He took it to the mill and had it ground for more meal. He never told Mama where he had been. Mama was afraid to ask. He was pretty drunk.

Sometime after that Mama found out he had stayed those two weeks in a hotel in Waynesville with a woman who Mama called a whore and had given her all our money.

We never got any new clothes for school. We had to wait till the Lions Club came to school before Christmas. Sometimes, we went hungry for days, but in school anyway we got free lunches.

* * *

One day Daddy took his moonshine to sell somewhere in Tennessee. When he got back, we saw he had bought himself a Jeep. He drove into the front yard in his Jeep. He was very proud of it. We didn't know how he got it home because he was so drunk that when he got out, he fell on the ground.

He said, "Look what I bought with my liquor money."

We were all happy to see the Jeep. Now we could all go to Waynesville. Daddy drove down the road in his Jeep and when he came back a short time later, he had a big sack of corn meal. We all knew he never took any corn to get it ground to meal and he was gone only around fifteen minutes.

Mama asked, "Who gave you the meal?"

"Never mind, just cook the damn stuff."

That "quick" bag of corn meal would come back to haunt him and cause our family all kinds of bad trouble.

* * *

Joe was out playing around the Jeep with this round ball kind of hammer. He hit the tire of the Jeep as hard as he could. The hammer bounced off the rubber tire and hit him in the head right between his eyes. He took off running as fast as he could. As he ran,

Moonshiner's Daughter

he stepped on an old broken jar and cut his foot wide open. He never went to the doctor. Cheryl and I took care of him. Mama fainted over when she looked at the bad gash. Joe had a knot between his eyes for days. Then it turned real black and blue.

Joe was always doing something to hurt himself. One day he had a hammer and nails. He drove all the nails through an old plank. After that, he got on the porch and jumped down onto that plank. One of the nails went all the way through his bare foot. Of course, he had no shoes on. He had to put his foot in a pail of hot water with salts in it for over a week to keep it from getting infected.

Mary Judith Messer

Daddy Nearly Dies &
The Stolen Necklace

Living so far out in the mountains, it was up to us to amuse ourselves and we got into lots of trouble wandering around like we did. I remember one summer day, Cheryl and I crossed a creek by walking across this log that went from one side to the other. Under the log, all along the creek grew plants we called stinging weeds. I got across the log okay and Cheryl came along behind me. She took a misstep and slid off the log and landed in those old stinging weeds. Even as fast as she could scamble out, they gave her blisters all over her whole body.

Those stinging weeds (stinging nettles) were a lot worse than blackberry briars. They made long welts even just barely touching them. Cheryl cried for hours. She was in a very sad shape. But that wasn't the last time I had a run in with stinging weed.

One day when we were in the tobacco field, Daddy unhitched Pat from her sled. He sat Joe and me on her big broad back and told us to ride her to the barn. We headed up the road bouncing along cause Joe made her trot. We trotted into the yard and there was a small creek by the house.

Joe said, "I'm going to make Old Pat jump the creek."

Just as we got to that creek, Old Pat stopped dead in her tracks, and threw Joe and me over her shoulders, right into that creek on our heads. I hit a rock and then landed on top of those stinging weeds, the worse thing I had ever been into. My arms, legs, back, every inch of my body had long welts. Joe never even got hurt, but I sure did. I had also cut my arm on a sharp rock. Me and horses just didn't get along. They have a mind of their own. When they do not want to do something, by golly, they don't do it. After that, I swore I would never ride a horse again.

* * *

Daddy took off in his Jeep before we got to ride in it and he didn't come back for over three months. We thought for sure he was dead. One morning we were going down the road to the bus stop and who do we see, but Daddy, walking…no Jeep. He had this jar of moonshine in his hand. The other arm was in a sling, made out of a white handkerchief tied around his neck with his arm in it. He was so drunk, he could barely walk, but he was sure holding on to that jar for dear life.

"Kids, you are very lucky to have a Daddy. I ran off of a Tennessee mountain and wrecked my Jeep. It was in a thousand pieces. I broke my arm and shoulder. I lay on them rocks for over a week. No one found me. I could not move."

We kids were so glad he had come back alive, but we couldn't wait around to find out what else had happened, we had to run to the bus stop. We stood at the bus stop half the morning, hoping against hope it hadn't already come and gone when we finally realized we had missed it. No good free lunch for us that day. Us three children had no choice but to trudge on home and it was twelve-thirty when we reached home. Mama was real surprised to see us coming back that late in the day. We had missed that bus lots of times and had to walk back home, but mostly we would see the bus going out of sight or just turning around. Even though we would run like the wind after it, often the driver would just keep going and we'd realize we had missed it and start for home right away.

Daddy was all piled up on the couch when we got home. Mama made us stay in the old barn loft so we would not wake him. She was afraid he would wake up mean drunk. When he did sober up, he told us he had lain on rocks after the Jeep wrecked and could not move. He told us his shoulder had bled and green flies had got on the wound and laid eggs, maggots were in his shoulder. He almost had gangrene. His arm and shoulder were in very bad shape.

Mary Judith Messer

He just stayed drunk so he could not feel the pain. But he did that anyway, stayed drunk, I mean.

Mama and us kids had to fend for ourselves most of the time anyway. He was always gone into the mountains or wherever. He also started cutting down these huge trees. He logged a lot. He slid the logs down the mountain. It was very hard work. One thing I can sure say about my Daddy, I did love him. He worked so hard at everything he did.

One summer day we all headed to the tobacco field and Daddy told Joe, "Go into the barn and get my tobacco knives off of the logs where I keep them. Get two of them. (This was the same kind of knife that Cheryl almost cut her leg off with.)

Joe came out of the barn carrying something, but it wasn't a tobacco knife. He had this huge copperhead snake around the neck. He had reached up on the log to get hold of the tobacco knife handle, but he did not get hold of a handle; he got hold of that snake. God was sure looking out for him that day. He just held on to that snake until he choked it to death. That was one scary snake.

* * *

One morning, on the way to school, someone had put an old metal pipe muffler on the school bus. All of a sudden, the girls in the back of the bus started screaming and jumped up on the bus seats. Then the whole bus load of kids began hollering.

Cheryl, Joe and I were sitting up front where the driver made us Longs sit every day. We couldn't tell what was going on except that by now every kid in the bus besides us were standing in their seats and screaming their heads off.

The bus driver pulled over to the side of the road, set the brake, and rushed to the back. "What in the hell is wrong with you kids?" he shouted. Then he saw what they saw and he stopped cold. One of the biggest copperheads you ever saw crawled out of that muffler. I will tell you the kids scrambled over each other and every seat to get out the door. For one time, I was very happy to be sitting in the front of the bus. I made one leap and I was out. Joe and

Cheryl were right behind me. The driver killed that thing and took it outside for everyone to see it was dead. As he held it up, we could see it was as long as the driver and he was a tall man.

* * *

On the school bus one morning, this Cole girl, sitting in the seat behind me, said to me, "Judith Long, you stole my locket! You need to give it back to me now."

I jerked my head around to look her in the eyes, thinking she was playing a trick or something. I saw she was dead serious.

"What are you talking about? I never even saw your locket. What does it look like?"

"You know what it looks like. You have it."

We argued all the way to school. By that time, the whole bus of kids were saying, "You have her locket. Give her back her locket."

She said, "If you don't give my locket back, I will go to the Principal's office."

I said, "Go ahead because I haven't ever seen that thing. You are just lying. You never had a locket in the first place."

When we got to school, I was in class when the teacher called me to her desk. She said, "Judith, go to the Principal's office."

I was not scared or anything because I knew I did not do anything or steal that girl's locket. I walked down the long hall and into the Principal's office. The Cole girl, Jane, sat in a chair. The Principal was behind his desk. He said "Come on in, Long. How you doing today?"

I replied, "Just fine."

He said, "We need to get right down to this. The reason why you are here in my office, Miss Cole here said you took her locket. Now all you need to do is give it back to her and we will all be okay."

"Sir, I have not got her locket. I have never seen it. I do not know even what it looks like…" I started to say more but he stopped me.

"Now, Miss Long, I will not sit here and listen to lies. You need to tell us the truth. Just give Miss Cole her locket or tell her

Mary Judith Messer

where you put it. I haven't time for all this foolishness. I will ask you only one more time, give Miss Cole her locket."

"But Sir, but Sir," I kept saying and he kept interrupting me.

"But Sir… I did not get it. Please."

By now I was very scared and I was shaking. I could see now that I had made a bad mistake. I had thought that when I told the principal the truth, which was I never got her locket, I would be okay and I would just be sent back to class.

He told my accuser, "Miss Cole, go on back to your room. Miss Long will give you back your locket."

Jane left the room. I was shocked when the Principal took me by the arm and pulled me over to him. Then he opened his desk drawer and pulled out a thick, thick leather strap. He then pushed me over his desk and hit me on the butt three times. My cotton dress got in the way so he pulled up the dress and hit me three more times.

"Now, Long, you want to tell me where the locket is?"

I was crying real hard. "Sir, I don't know where it is."

He pushed me again over his desk. My dress was still up, he swung that strap real hard and hit me six more times. By now my butt was in blisters and I was screaming.

"Long, where is Miss Cole's locket?"

I could hardly answer I was crying so hard. I finally got out, "I don't know."

He hit me six more hard licks.

I was hurting so very bad and I could not talk because snot was running down my face. I nodded my head up and down.

He stopped. "Okay that is more like it. Okay. Where is it?"

I could not talk; tears and snot were all running down my face into my mouth. I was choking on my own spit.

"Okay. Stop this crying and tell me where the locket is!"

I stood just choking on my spit. I could not get out any words and the harder I tried the worse it was.

"Okay", he said again. "Where is the locket?"

"I.. I.. I don't know."

He stood glaring at me. "You don't know?" he said. "You don't know? Get out of my office!"

Moonshiner's Daughter

I turned to leave, but I could hardly move, my backside hurt so badly. It took me about five minutes to walk to the door. I eased down the hall and went to the rest room. Safe inside, I twisted around to see my hips and butt. They felt like they were covered in big blisters. They were and they were busted. I stayed in the bathroom in one of the stalls which I had locked so no one would see me. I lay down on my side and curled up into a ball. Lying on the cold floor felt good on my blisters.

I lay on the floor for a long time. Some kids came in. I heard them talking about catching the bus. I crawled up on my knees and pulled up on the toilet to get up. When I finally got on my feet, I could hardly stand because I was in such pain. I was so sure I was dying. I finally got out of the bathroom, still hurting so bad, when I saw Cheryl coming down the hall.

She called out, "Hurry up. We'll miss the bus!"

When she saw me all bent over and barely walking, she ran to me. "What happened to you?"

I told her the Principal beat me up.

She said, "That old son of a bitch. I will get Daddy to shoot him."

When we did get to the bus, every one shouted out the windows at us, "We are all on and waiting for y'uns." Joe had begged the bus driver not to leave us. Cheryl helped me up the steps of the open door of the bus. We got to our seat but I could not sit down.

The bus driver said, "Okay, Long, anytime. Get in that seat. We cannot take off till you are in that seat."

I tried to sit but the pain was too bad.

The driver was very mad by now. He told me that he would go get the Principal. I turned around and put my knees in the seat first. I eased myself in the seat.

The driver finally started up. I rode all the way to the bus stop on my knees. The kids made fun of me all the way. I tried not to see them. I shut my eyes. Joe and Cheryl were almost in a fight with them. We finally got to our stop. Cheryl helped me out of the bus. As we stepped down the bus steps, the bus driver said, "What in hell happened to her?"

Mary Judith Messer

Cheryl didn't say a word.

Joe was behind us. He said, "That g--damn Principal beat her up." and he jumped out of the bus.

You talk about a bad time. I sure had it, trying to walk the long way from the bus stop to the shack. Without Cheryl and Joe helping me, I would never have made it. I would take a few steps and stop, take a few steps and stop. It took us 2 1/2 hours to get home. When we got in sight of the shack, we saw Mama standing out on the porch with her hands full of apple tree limbs.

Joe turned me loose and ran to tell Mama why we were so late.

She dropped the limbs and came to us. When she raised my dress, she almost fainted. The leather strap had made blisters and burst them. My butt and hips were raw and bleeding.

Mama got to shaking so bad, she could not be still. She was so mad, she went to school the next day. She got someone with an auto at the Lance's house that lived past our bus stop to take her. These Lances were kin to the ones that lived above us.

Cheryl and Joe came back and told me Mama slapped the Principal and two teachers had to pull her off of him.

I never went back that school year. Before long, Joe and Cheryl both got belted by that same principal. He sure had it in for us Longs.

Two days after my beating Cheryl told me, "The bus driver was sweeping out the bus yesterday and he found the locket." He turned it into the principal and that's how Jane Cole got her locket back.

Daddy Goes To Prison &
The Rolling Store Visits

A few months later, two law cars drove up the old dirt road. We saw them as they rounded the turn. We were playing with our dolls. Cheryl and I ran in the shack to tell Mama. Daddy was drunk in the barn loft.

The law man said, "Is this Terry Long's house?"

Mama came out on the little porch. She said, "Yes. What is it?"

He said, "We just need to see Terry."

Mama said, "Joe, run out to the loft for your Daddy."

Joe was gone in a flash and we saw Daddy come down the ladder. He went over to the lawmen. "What's going on?" Daddy asked.

The lawman said, "We have a warrant for your arrest."

"What for?"

One of them stepped forward with a piece of paper. He reached out and handed it to Daddy. Daddy looked at it, then handed it up to Mama. She looked at it and said, "Terry, it says here that you stole a sack of meal from in front of Lowman's mail box. Did you steal it?"

Daddy looked at her. "Hell no!" By now he was somewhat sobered up after sleeping it off in the barn hay.

I remembered Daddy going out and bringing back that sack of ground meal a few months before when Mama had questioned him. We thought somebody must have given it to him at the time.

It was a custom in those parts that people sometimes set tow sacks of dried corn by the mail boxes and the mailmen would pick them up and drop them off at the grist mill to be ground into cornmeal. The next day, the mailman would leave the sacks of meal back at the mail boxes.

"Well, Terry," one of the law men said, "we are going to have to take you in." They put two pairs of handcuffs on him. Daddy had pretty big arms so they put two pairs together so the cuffs would reach.

All us kids ran around the cars, screaming, "Please don't take our Daddy to jail!" We took sticks and rocks and hit those two law cars. The law men just drove off without a word taking our Daddy with them.

Two weeks after they had arrested Daddy, Mama got a ride with the mail man to town. By the time she got to the Waynesville Courthouse, he had already been tried and sentenced to two years in federal prison for stealing a sack of corn meal. I also think that they must have found his still.

* * *

Now you think we were in bad shape before? Nothing will beat what happened to us next. Mama went to see Daddy before they sent him off and he told her to go up to Jess Welch's house and have him check to see if they had cut down his still or not.

Mama came home and made Joe and Cheryl walk the mountains to find Jess's house, way up in the woods, almost to the Cataloochee Park line, to tell him to stop at our shack. Tell him, "I need to talk to him," she said.

They were gone for four hours and it was black dark when we saw them. We had this old dog named Brownie. We heard him barking and ran out to see them. They said they got lost, but finally found Jess's house.

Cheryl said, "He will be by tomorrow."

Jess was good for his word. He was at the shack early.

Mama told him what Daddy wanted. Jess must have known where the still was because he did not ask us to take him to it.

Moonshiner's Daughter

The next day our Brownie dog was in the grass beside the old rock chimney. We heard him yelp and Joe ran to him. A big copperhead was crawling away. Joe got a rock, but it got away.

Old Brownie had been with us for as long as I could remember. And now, he had been bitten on the side of his face right below his eye. Poor old thing, he just lay around for days. He was an old dog, but the bite made him not even bark. His face was swollen up so big, he never looked like old Brownie. We kids were all sad. We thought old Brownie would die, but he didn't. Every time it rained, though, his face swelled up as big as a pumpkin.

* * *

One day Mama was down at Florence Shelly's shack where she went pretty often. She liked her a lot. She came home and told us that Florence was going to tell Grady Honeycutt to come to the mail boxes with his Rolling Store so we could come down and buy some groceries.

She told Mama he would come every Tuesday at 4PM. We were to be at the mail box if we wanted anything.

Mama was now getting $40.00 a month from the Welfare Department since Daddy was in prison. We went down the long road to the mail boxes Tuesday at 3 o'clock. We wanted to make sure we did not miss the Rolling Store. Mama made us all go so we could help carry home all the groceries.

We all waited at the mail boxes bus stop for the Rolling Store. Florence was down with us. Just what a sight us children saw. This big thing came up the road. It was only a little smaller than our school bus, but it was made differently. It was white where our bus was orange. It turned around where the school bus turned and stopped.

Joe was already to the steps when Mama told us to stand back and let Florence in first. Joe was already inside. When we did get to the door, we could not believe our eyes. It had shelf after shelf of all kinds of canned food, bags of beans, corn meal, flour, sugar, salt and

Mary Judith Messer

jars of hard candy, but what I set my eyes on were the bananas. I just loved bananas. I thought *I could eat a hundred without stopping.*

Mama bought a bag of sugar, flour, dried beans and a piece of fat back. She got some canned food and a bag of salt, a loaf of bread and she handed her welfare check to Grady.

He added up all her food and put it in several bags. Then he handed Joe two bags, Cheryl two bags, and me, two bags. There was one small bag for Joanie. I never wanted to leave the Rolling Store. It was more food than I had ever seen in my whole life. Us kids had never even been in a grocery store, so you can imagine what kind of surprise that Rolling Store was.

Mama had us all going out the door when she stopped and turned around. She picked up a bright yellow bunch of the bananas, paid for them and Grady put them in a bag.

I was the happiest girl in the world. Now, Mama had a bag to carry. We walked up the road with Florence to her little house. Then we had almost a mile to go before I could get home and make me a banana sandwich.

When we got home Mama said, "I forgot the chicken feed. We will have to feed the chickens corn bread till next Tuesday when Grady comes back." She sent us over to Jim Frank's house to get some corn.

Jim and Lulu had one boy named Gerald. He was older than the Long's kids. We were invited into the kitchen. Jim and Gerald were sitting at the kitchen table.

Cheryl and I just stood there, looking at that table full of food. There was a big bowl of soup beans, a bowl of young baked potatoes with butter all over the top, a big cake of corn bread, some okra and some boiled ears of corn, sliced cucumbers and some young green onions. There was a print of homemade butter and a gallon jar of buttermilk. Was I hungry! My mouth just watered. I knew Cheryl was hungry also. We had not eaten all day.

Lulu said, "Jim, these girls need some corn to feed their chickens."

He said, "I will get you some when I finish eating. I'll have to go up to the barn."

Moonshiner's Daughter

"You girls hungry?" She asked. "Have you had your supper?"

At the same time, we say, "No, we haven't eaten supper, and yes, we are hungry."

Jim said, "Well Lulu, fix them a plate for they can sit on the end of the table."

Lulu gave us two plates and we sat down, too bashful to reach for any food, so Lulu picked up a bowl of food, one at a time, and let us dip out of each bowl all the food we wanted.

Jim talked to us some about us being real careful about the snakes. Also he talked about bears and them panthers. He said, "I know your dad's gone so you older girls will have to watch out for the young 'uns."

We had our mouths so full of all the good food it took us a while to chew and swallow before we could answer him, "We do watch out for Joe and Joanie."

Afterwards, Jim took us up to his barn where he had a silo full of corn. He gave us some in a sack. He had some cows, chickens, pigs, everything a farmer would want. There was a nice corn field and a garden. Jim had this snuff he put in his jaws. Sometimes you would see it all over his lips. He was a hard worker, and a very good man. All of the Franks were. Our Mama dipped snuff also and sometimes we had to borrow snuff for her.

On Tuesday, Mama gave us some money. It was about $2.00. She sent Joe, Cheryl and me to the bus stop to wait for the Rolling Store. She told us to be sure not to forget the sack of chicken feed. She made us a list of everything we were to get. We did not see Florence anywhere. We stopped at the Old Road and hollered for her, but she never came out so we walked on to the bus stop where we waited for a long time.

Cheryl said, "I think he is late. For sure, it is after 5 o'clock, because the sun has gone down."

Finally we saw him turning around. He said, "Sorry kids. I had some car trouble."

Mary Judith Messer

We handed him our list and he got all the things on it and put them on his little counter. We paid him, but we were short a dollar and twenty-five cents.

"That's okay, kids. Anytime you don't have the money, I will put it in my book and you can pay me next month when your Mother gets her check."

We thanked him. Cheryl and I got bags of food, sugar, flour and all and we let Joe carry the bag of chicken feed. We told him after he got tired, we each would carry it some. By now it was getting pretty dark. We tried to walk fast, but Joe was walking behind and could not keep up.

We told him, "Hurry up! Hurry up!", but he seemed to get slower and slower. We were getting afraid and thought we heard things in the old log barn as we passed and I wanted to go faster. We heard something in the woods that sounded like something running. By now, Cheryl and I were scared crazy.

All at once, we saw something with red eyes and it was coming up the road behind us. We started out running; Joe began to catch up to us. We ran faster. We could make out a big long black thing. It looked like a big black cat, but it was huge. We never stopped to look back again, but we heard this thing as it screamed like a baby dying.

We threw down everything we have. Joe had already thrown the chicken feed down and had passed us like a puff of wind. We got home and Mama was happy we were alive, but unhappy about our missing food.

The next day we all went to the road to find our food. When we got to the spot where we dropped it, chicken feed was everywhere. All the food was torn up. The loaf bread was gone, the paper sacks were laying scattered around into long shreds. Something with very sharp claws had torn it up. Mama asked Jess Welch when we saw him the next day, "What could that have been?"

He said, "A black panther. These woods are full of them. Try not to be out after dark. You need to keep the kids where you can see them."

Moonshiner's Daughter

"They have to walk to the bus stop all the time. Will a panther attack them?" asked Mama.

He said, "Tell them to always make lots of noise when they walk. It would be good to have a tin can and take a stick and beat it. Maybe it will scare away a bear or a panther. Terry sure needs to be here with his family."

You could say that again.

This was the old Rolling Store bus, or what was left of it when I took the picture. It fed lots of hungry kids who lived in the "sticks" in its good old days, including us!

Mary Judith Messer

From Bad To Worse & Coon Hunting

Jack and Zeb, the two teenage neighbors of ours, started coming around. Mama would wind up her old record player. She had lots of country records. That man that went with her and Lucie Ann to Nashville bought them for her. She would turn the handle on her record player to wind it up, put a record on and the boys and Mama would dance up a storm. We kids would just watch them. It was fun, a good time, but when they would go way into the night, we kids would get sleepy and want to sleep and their racket kept us all awake. The next day, we could not get up on time and we had to run all the way to get to the bus stop just to find it was gone and left us.

Mama and those boys were drinking. I think they drank Daddy's moonshine. They all were drunk. Those boys ate everything in the house, all our light bread, bananas, just everything. Before the week was up, we almost starved to death, but Mama let them do it all the time. They knew when we got our food and here they would come even though they had all kinds of food at home. I went to their house one time for Mama to borrow a cup of sugar. I saw cows, horses, a corn patch, big gardens, a pretty nice house, nothing like our shack. I saw the crippled boy. He was a big boy, but his legs went back in a circle. He crawled out on the porch. I didn't know why he couldn't walk.

Sometimes when Mama and those boys were dancing and drunk, Mama and one of them would climb up the ladder into the attic. Nothing was up there, but old wooden rafters and planks lying on top of the rafters; I knew that because Joe and I had climbed up there before. Mama and the boys would make all kinds of funny sounds up in that loft. When one of the boys came down, another would go up. They did this a lot.

* * *

We found out they were going to bring Daddy back to the Haywood County Jail. They were going to try him for moonshining again.

We saw a bunch of Jeep trucks go up the old wagon road, but had no idea who it was. We found out later it was the revenuers. Somehow they had found another still that wasn't Daddy's and cut it down. It wasn't his, but they had Mama go to the court house the next day and she was told by Jess Welch that they were going to try him.

She hoped to see him at 10 o'clock but she never knew if he got her message or not. Mama never let any of us kids go with her. Jess took her. She got back and told us Daddy got three more years, and they were going to send him to Florida to the Federal Prison in Tallahassee.

We were all very sad, but what could we do? We had to make out the best we could. Uncle Paul found out where we had moved to and on a Saturday night in he popped. He had this woman with him, and also another couple. They had plenty of store-bought whisky with them. They all stayed for over a week and drank one drink after another. They had enough whisky to last a week and a half. When it was gone, they were gone.

We kids sure were glad. They almost got into fights and Cheryl and I had to carry water in the dark. All that dancing stopped till them Lances were back.

One night Joe sat down on one of Mama's old 78's records. They were made of this real hard plastic. Joe got up and the record was broken. Mama was so very mad. When I picked it up out of the chair and showed it to her she said, "Take the rest of that record and beat him over the head."

Mary Judith Messer

Maybe she was just kidding but I took the piece of broken record and hit him. The blood went everywhere, down his face, in his ears, all over.

Mama started screaming, "You have killed him!" She just kept screaming.

Cheryl grabbed a hand towel and put it around his head. In a minute the towel was soaked in blood. Then she got another one and wet it in a bucket of water. She got the blood stopped. It was a small gash on top of his head.

Mama grabbed the broom stick and beat me till it broke. I could not stand up. Then she grabbed the stick she kept by the cook stove that she stirred the fire up with. I came an inch of dying that night. Joe and Cheryl both screamed for her to stop. My whole body was covered with black and blue bruises.

* * *

One night she was very drunk, the boys had been down dancing and eating. They were all drunk. Cheryl and us were trying to get to sleep because school was the next day. Mama told Cheryl and me to get up. We wanted to know why she wanted us to get up.

She said, "Don't ask questions, just get the hell up. "

I got up but Cheryl was real slow; she finally stumbled into the kitchen, still half asleep.

Mama said, "Who the hell do you think you are not coming when I call you?" She had this butcher knife in her hand and I saw it right away. Cheryl didn't notice it. All of a sudden, she grabbed Cheryl by the hair and held the sharp knife to her throat. She zipped it across her throat and made blood come out her throat from one ear to the other.

I was crying, "Please Mama, please don't kill her. Put the knife down."

Mama let go of her hair and Cheryl fell to the floor. Mama was still holding the knife. "I am going to kill both of you," she screamed.

Moonshiner's Daughter

Cheryl crawled past her and jumped up. We both ran out into the dark night. We ran down below the old barn and hid in the Frank's tobacco patch in the tall plants. We were afraid to go into the barn thinking she may come in and find us. All night, we huddled up in that tobacco field. We could feel a snake crawl over our legs but we were as still as we could be. We lay on each other the rest of the night. When daylight came, we could hear Mama calling us. We came out of the tobacco field and walked to the house. Cheryl had a small bloody cut across her throat.

Mama said, "You all have missed the bus again. It's 8 o'clock." She never said one word about the knife or why we stayed out all night.

* * *

On the school bus one afternoon, I noticed that Simon Smith had missed his bus stop. He just stayed in his seat, next to one of the Lance boys. Simon was around sixteen. The Lance boy was Jack Lance, he was seventeen. Cheryl, Joe and I got off of the bus at our stop. Joe ran on up the road; he always ran ahead to try to beat us home. We turned around and Jack and Simon were walking behind us. They were talking low so we could not hear what they were saying. We were almost to the old log barn, about a quarter mile from Florence's house. Simon caught up to us and said to Cheryl, "Hey, do you want to see something real funny?"

Cheryl said, "Like what?"

He said, "It is in that old barn. Come on, I will show it to you."

I looked at Cheryl and wondered what he was going to show her. Then Jack also told her, "Come on, we want to show you something."

Before I knew just what had happened, they grabbed her arms and over the bank they went into the old barn. I think *it better not be a snake they are going to scare her with.*

After just a minute, I heard Cheryl start screaming. I began running up and down the road. I was shouting all the bad cuss words

Mary Judith Messer

I have ever heard Mama and Daddy say and I started throwing rocks at the old barn.

Cheryl kept on crying and screaming but I was afraid to get any closer to the barn. After a few minutes, I saw Jack, with Simon right behind him, running out of the side door.

I ran down to the barn and found Cheryl lying on the old dirt floor, her panties laying on the dirt beside her. She had blood all over her legs and she was crying real bad. She got up and went down to the creek. She dipped her panties in the water and washed off the blood. She was still crying so hard she could not see. She begged me, "Please don't tell Mama. She will kill me."

"What did they do to you, Cheryl? Tell me," I begged. I had no idea what had happened to her. I had seen Mama go up in the loft with them boys and I heard all the noise and I had seen Mama and Daddy in bed wiggling once, but I didn't know what they were doing.

She said, "Both of those boys put their pee pee in me." Cheryl was sore for weeks. She could hardly walk. I knew Joe had a pee pee and it wasn't like us girls.

* * *

We kids had to walk to the bus stop even when it snowed. We would walk all the way down, just to find out there was no school. When it was slick, the bus wouldn't run on the icy dirt roads. We went to the bus stop lots of times just to have to walk back home in the ice or snow.

Cheryl came down very sick. She was in bed for two weeks and did not get any better. Then Joe and I got sick. All three of us were in bed for a long time. Mama told Florence we were bad sick. Florence had buried her mother and we never even knew she had even died. Florence told Mama, "You better get yourself to the doctor with those kids."

Cheryl was getting worse so Mama got Jess to take us to the doctor. She had to take all of us. She took us to Dr. Stringfield and he said, "Cheryl has got Rheumatic Fever. Joe and Judith have

Moonshiner's Daughter

Scarlet Fever. This fever Cheryl has will weaken her heart. When these kids are out in the snow and cold weather, they need warm clothing."

Cheryl never had shoes half the time and neither did I. He gave us lots of different kinds of medicine and Jess took us home. We were some very sick kids for a long time. We missed so much of school that we never passed to the next grade.

Those old Lance boys were still coming around. After we got well, Mama let them start coming back. One night Jack and Zeb came down. She asked them if they wanted to hear some music. She started to put a record on, but Jack said, "Emily, we are going coon hunting. Can Cheryl come with us?"

Mama looked at Cheryl then back at the boys and said, "Okay. She can go."

"Cheryl, go with Jack and Zeb coon hunting." Then she said, "Judith, you go with them too."

"But Mama, it is dark and cold," I said.

"That's the best time to coon hunt," Zeb said.

If Mama had known a thing about coon hunting, she would have known you have to take a dog with you. Jack and Zeb had no dog. Even I knew that much. You do not coon hunt without a dog.

She made me go on with them and off we went into the woods. We didn't get too far before Jack and Zeb got Cheryl off behind a big log. I couldn't see them because it was too dark, but I could hear Cheryl crying. I just stood behind a big tree, afraid to move in case it would have drawn attention to myself. Years later, I often puzzled why they didn't rape me, too. Even though I probably only weighed about seventy pounds, I would have fought them like the devil if they had tried that with me.

About a week after this, they came down again. Cheryl begged Mama not to make her go. "I don't like to coon hunt, Mama, please don't make me go."

"I don't like it either!" I told Mama.

Even though we put up a big fuss, in the end, Mama made us go. They did the same thing to Cheryl again. She cried and told them to stop, but her cries did not matter. *There was no one to help.*

Mary Judith Messer

Thinking back on that bad time, I have often wondered if Mama knew what was happening to Cheryl. It's a hard thing to believe your mother was a party to her own daughter's rape, but maybe that was just part of her insanity. I thank God and Jesus that I was too young for their attention. Cheryl was only thirteen.

A Terrible Winter & Papaw Dies

The first summer that Daddy was in prison, it was not too bad on Cheryl and me, but in the winter, it was pure hell. We had to take this old cross cut saw and walk in the deep snow up in the woods. We had to saw up logs for our firewood so we would not freeze to death. Our hands and feet would be so cold; we lost all feeling in them. After we got the blocks cut, we had to roll them all the way to the shack. They looked like huge snow balls when we got them to the shack. Then we had to knock the snow off and bust the big blocks with an ax. We had to chop the block about twenty five times before it would bust. After we finally got it cut up, we then had to carry it in the shack.

We were so cold that when we started to get warm inside, we hurt all over. When the snow got so high up over Cheryl and my waist, Mama made us go to the barn and start sawing up the big logs the barn and stable were made of. Cheryl and I sawed up so much of that barn, it was a wonder it never fell down.

Mama got a message from someone that her Daddy had got killed in Spartanburg, South Carolina. Our Papaw was dead.

Mama got Jess Welch to drive us to South Carolina. I got so sick on those winding roads out of Foggy Creek, Mama gave me a jar to throw up in, and the first time I used it I filled it full. Half of us kids were on the back of Jess's truck and every time I looked up at the winding road, I got sicker. The wind in my hair and face made me feel some better. I just shut my eyes and let the wind blow in my face. Cheryl was riding in the back with me. She never got sick. The young ones rode in the front of the truck with Mama and Jess.

It was a very long ride to South Carolina. We were so tired by the time we got there. Joe and Joanie had slept half the way, but not Cheryl and me. I was always watching out so we wouldn't wreck.

We got to this house in Spartanburg and some woman lived there that was a friend to our Papaw. She let us all get into this bed. It was real late at night when we got to her house. We woke up the next morning when this lady called us up to a table full of eggs, biscuits, grits, gravy and a bowl of peaches. We ate our fill. We kids tried to hear what she told Mama about our Papaw.

"You know they cannot find his left leg," she said.

We could not make sense out of what she said. Our Papaw never had a wooden leg, he walked just fine. "Where is Papaw? We want to see him. We want him to give us some gum," we told her.

Mama was crying and we just didn't understand why she was crying.

Around dinner time, three men in real nice suits and neck ties came into the house. When I saw them I said to myself, *Papaw dresses like them. He had a suit and tie on when we saw him.*

The men had this long, long box. They sat it on this high thing. Us kids were too short to see the top of it. Then one of the men opened the lid. When he did, Mama let out a holler. She was already crying and now, she got worse. We could not see in the box. It was a real pretty box. It was all shiny with gold and silver.

After the men left, I asked Mama, "What did they bring in that box?"

"Honey, it is your Papaw."

I jumped up and down, and so did Joe and Joanie. I don't think Joanie could remember him, but Joe, Cheryl and I sure did. Joanie was too young when he came to see us.

"Mama, Mama, why is he sleeping in that funny bed? Wake him up. I want to see him." I cried.

"Kids, he is dead and will not wake up."

We didn't understand. She put a chair up next to the box. First she helped me in the chair. "Kiss your Papaw good bye," she said.

Moonshiner's Daughter

I saw him lying in that big box. He looked so good with his tie and jacket, but he was asleep. To me he looked white, real white.

"Papaw. Papaw, wake up," but he didn't wake up.

"Kiss your Papaw goodbye," Mama told me again.

I put my lips on his jaw. He was so cold and did not move. I started screaming and screaming and I could not stop. Mama lifted me down from the chair. The lady whose house we were staying at took me into the kitchen and set me on her lap and rocked and rocked me. She sang a song to me, but I could not hear her. She was so nice. I will always remember her. I can hear Cheryl and Joe crying. We cried all day.

Mama put us outside. "Play out in the sunshine and stop crying."

That night we all had to go to sleep with our Papaw laying in the other room in that box. The next day we put him in the cold, dark ground.

We never saw Uncle Paul. I don't know if he knew his Daddy was dead. The woman told Mama that our Papaw was drunk and was walking on the highway in Spartanburg when a big log truck hit him and knocked him way down the road. He had a bottle of whisky in his vest pocket and it broke into a million little pieces.

She said, "You and Paul have some insurance money coming. I will mail you your check. When you see Paul, tell him to get hold of me and I will mail his to him."

We kids had never seen so many cars and big buildings. We had been with Daddy one time to Asheville, but we only went to the Tobacco Warehouse. We never got to see all the stores and all. It would have been a fun trip to South Carolina if we weren't so sad.

Jess took us back to the mountains to our little shack. After seeing some of the world, I went around daydreaming of all the pretty houses, nice cars, and all.

Two days later, Cheryl and I were up in the woods with the old cross cut saw. We were trying to find some logs laying down so we could saw them for stove wood. We saw Jess Welch and Lester Lance.

Jess said, "You girls getting wood?"

Mary Judith Messer

Cheryl answered, "Yes. We got to get some before dark."

Jess took the saw and said, "Over here, Judith, is a nice log. Come help me saw it up. Cheryl can go with Lester to find some more logs."

I walked over to where Jess was and he set the blade to the log. I got hold of one handle and he got the other one. Cheryl went off with Lester . We cut a few licks when I heard Cheryl cry out. She was almost screaming.

"What's Lester doing to her?" She just kept on screaming and I started to run up in the woods where they were. Jess pulled me back and said, "Stay here. I will see what is wrong with her."

He disappeared up in the woods. I heard her still crying. She finally came into sight and was crying real bad. Lester was behind her and Jess was behind him. Jess was Lester's uncle and Lester was a lot older than Cheryl or myself. Jess took Lester down through the woods and out of sight. Cheryl had blood all over her cotton dress. She was still crying.

"Cheryl, what did Lester do to you?"

"He tried to put his real big pee pee in me. He could not get it in and it hurts so bad."

Mama wanted to know where our firewood was. I don't know why she never saw all that blood on Cheryl's dress. She could not walk for a week or longer, but Mama made her do her work just the same.

Those boys were still coming down now and then.

The New Washer & Learning To Steal

A few months after our Papaw died, Mama got a good idea. She took me with her to catch the mailman. She told me, "Cheryl can watch Joanie and Joe. You are going with me. We are going to town in Waynesville."

We all knew she got a check from the woman in South Carolina, her part of the insurance money. She never told us how much money she got.

Mama and I rode the mail wagon to Waynesville. I got a little sick on them old winding roads when we came out, but I never vomited.

Once there, the mailman let us out on Main Street and we started walking past all these stores. There was a hardware store, Smith's Drug Store, the Curb Market, a 5 & 10 cent store, and others. We kept going up the street but I was so excited I skipped. Mama led me into this store where I saw all kinds of real new furniture. A man saw us enter and walked over to us. His name was Mr. Massie. This was his store. "Ma'am, what can I do for you?"

"I need to see some washing machines," Mama said.

"Right this way. We have lots of them."

We followed him over to this corner and saw all the washing machines.

They were all round and white with rollers on top. Mama picked out one and asked the price.

Mr. Massie said, "That one is $75.00."

Mama said, "I will take it, but I do not know how I will get it to Foggy Creek."

Mr. Massie said, "Don't worry. We will take it for you." Mama asked him what time could he take it?

"We can bring it anytime. I will call my man. We'll get it loaded up."

Mama gave Mr. Massie her insurance check and he made change for her. She told him we needed a ride back to Foggy Creek, but we needed to go to Clyde Ray's Grocery Store first.

"Why sure," he said. "Do you need an hour to get your groceries?"

"That will be fine." We walked out of the furniture store and down the hill to the grocery store. It was the same store that always bought Mama's black walnut kernels. We got all our groceries and stood in the front of the store to watch for Mr. Massie's truck with our brand new washing machine.

"I see him!" I told Mama. We started to carry out our bags of groceries but the man came in to help because we had big bags of food and we also had a bag of chicken feed. Everything I asked for, Mama got it. We rode back to Foggy Creek, both of us grinning from ear to ear. It was one of the happiest days of my life.

Joe and Cheryl were glad to see us. Cheryl was excited about the new washer. Now she wouldn't have to help Mama with that old wash board.

Mama let the delivery man set her new washer on the small back porch. We knew we would still have to carry all the water to do the wash, but it would be lots easier on Mama and Cheryl.

Except for one thing. Washing machines needed electricity to work and we didn't have any at that old shack. No electricity. Seventy-five dollars was a lot of money back then for something we couldn't even use. Mama just couldn't stop laughing the next day every time she thought about what she had done. Even so, it sure looked nice sitting on the back porch.

* * *

Uncle Paul and a couple of friends came up one Saturday night. Mama told him about his Daddy, our Papaw. He got the

Moonshiner's Daughter

couple with him to turn right around and take him at once to Spartanburg to pick up his check. He was very drunk and so was the couple. We don't know if they got to South Carolina. They were so drunk.

One night them Lance boys came down. They ate some of our food, as usual, and Mama asked if they wanted her to put on a record and dance.

They said, "No. We are going coon hunting."

Zeb said, "We want Cheryl to go with us."

Mama looked over at Cheryl and asked, "Cheryl, do you want to go with them?"

She had never asked Cheryl before, did she want to go with them, she had just said, "Go." I think Mama must have known about Lester or something, but she never said not a word about it.

Cheryl said, "No, Mama. No! Don't make me go. I don't want to go coon hunting."

Mama looked at Zeb and then at Jack. "She don't want to go and I am not going to make her."

The times before Mama was drunk when she made Cheryl go and made me go also. This time, she was drinking, but she was not drunk. Zeb and Jack left the shack and slammed the door so hard we thought it would come off its hinges.

We were all in bed sound asleep that night when all of a sudden, we heard rocks raining down on top of our tin roof. Scared to death, we all jumped out of bed screaming. We ran to Mama, the noise from the rocks about made us deaf. Joanie was screaming so bad and Mama was trying to cover her ears with her hands. It never stopped for a good long time. Finally it got quiet. We heard some snickering and laughing outside. Mama peeped out and saw Zeb and Jack high tailing it up the old dirt road. For almost a week, every night, they did the same thing. For the rest of the time we lived in that old shack, at dark, when there was a full moon, we could look up from our bed to the roof and it was like stars were on the ceiling. We had so many holes in the tin roof that when it rained we had to set buckets and jars all over the shack to catch the water. It also rained on our beds.

Mary Judith Messer

* * *

Mama started to take me to town once a month. We always rode out with the mail wagon. Cheryl had to keep the two younger kids. We went up the street to the 5 & 10 cent store where I would see all these nice brand new little dresses, shoes, coats and candy. It was just too much to take in. I never knew one place could have so many good things.

Mama told me, "Watch me."

I did and she was looking all around the store, then she picked something up and put it in her purse. Then, she went on down the aisle in the store, looked all around again and did the same thing. Mama came up close to me and whispered, "Now, you do it, but put whatever you want under your sweater."

I told her, "But Mama, that's stealing."

She gave me one of her real bad looks. I almost sank into my shoes.

She said, "You want nice things don't you? Then get them."

The first time I tried to put a scarf under my sweater, I was so afraid, I shook all over. I couldn't be still.

Mama grabbed me by the arm and turned my arm around and shoved me out the door of the store. She didn't let go of my arm. I cried, "Mama. it hurts, it hurts."

Outside, she jerked me up against the block building, hit me in the face and said, "I am going to beat your ass good when we get home."

I cried, "Mama, I am scared."

She said, "Shut that damn crying up. We are going in the other 5 & 10 cent store and you better do it right this time. Watch everywhere and get you and Cheryl some panties." I did this time as I was told, but I never looked at the sizes of the socks or panties. I just snatched them and shoved them under my sweater.

We would leave all our bags of things with a man at his little store. The man was blind, but he had this little store on Main Street beside a taxi stand. Mama asked him could she leave all her bags in a safe place out of the way in his store.

He said, "Just put them in the corner over there."

So every time we came to town, we left all our things in that corner. We knew they would be safe. The blind man could hear real good. He knew as soon as anyone stepped in the door. Sometimes Mama left me to watch after the things while she went around the stores. She took me to town with her every time. We took a taxi back from town each time.

I ask Cheryl to beg Mama to let her go with her. I would watch after Joe and Joanie.

But Mama always told Cheryl no. She always said, "You stay with the kids. Judith is going with me." We both knew better than to argue with her. She could get real mean if we did not mind.

Two days before Christmas, Mama took me to town again. She told that blind man, "Judith is going to watch our bags" and off she went.

As soon as she walked out the door, the old man started asking me all kinds of things like "How old are you? Where do you live? Where is your Daddy?" Lots of questions. I was sitting on one of the stools in front of his counter. He asked, "Do you want a dope?" (That's what we called soda pop.)

I told him, "I don't have the money." Of all the times I had been in his little store, he had never talked to me, not even to just say "Hello". Now he asked, "Do you want a dope?"

"It's okay. You don't have to pay. It's free."

I thought *how can he give away free drinks?* There was a sign on the drink machine that read 5 cents.

He got a soda and sat it on the counter for me. Right then, a man came into the store that the blind man knew. The man asked for a can of chewing tobacco. When he said the kind he wanted, my eyes filled with tears because it made me think of my Daddy. The man had overalls on just like my Daddy, too. He got his tobacco and went out.

Of all the times I had been in this store, he was the only person I had seen come in.

Mary Judith Messer

The blind man started walking around the counter, feeling his way with one hand on the counter. He came to the stool where I was sitting. He reached out and felt my shoulder, then patted me on my back, then put his hand on my head and patted my head. He said, "What a nice girl you are. I bet you are sure pretty. What color is your hair?"

I told him. Then he asked, "What color are your eyes?" He kept on talking all the time with his hand on me. Now he put it on my leg and started rubbing my leg.

I wiggled a little and he said, "It's okay. You know I love you." Then he slid his hand under my cotton dress. I knew what he was up to and tried to slide off the stool. He had me by the arm and was trying to put his hand in my panties.

"You want another dope, or how about some ice cream?"

I twisted off the stool and lost my balance, falling to the floor. My feet couldn't touch the floor because the stool was too high, so I fell. He was feeling around for me. I scooted real quiet over to where the door was, next to our bags. I stayed real still so he would not know where I was.

He felt around his counter and walked back over behind his counter. He did not speak to me again. I was very happy and waited in the corner as quiet as I could.

Not too long after that, Mama came in with more bags. I dared never say one word to her about the old, blind man.

Every few weeks Mama made me go back to town with her. She told me one more time, for me to stay with her things in the blind man's store.

I told her, "Mama, I don't want to."

She hit me in the mouth and blood went everywhere.

She said, "Stay and if you see anything you want, like crackers or candy, get you and the kids some."

I stayed in the corner, then I saw a carton full of caramel popcorn and I got four boxes, one for each of us kids. I tried to be very quiet. I saw the old blind man take his hand and run it around his counter. He was walking all around his store and came to the carton with the caramel popcorn in it. He stopped and felt all the

Moonshiner's Daughter

boxes and said, "I have to go to the toilet." He went out the door and came back in a few minutes. He went around behind his counter and was feeling all over again.

A few minutes passed and in walked two men in uniform. They were policeman. I was so scared, I was crying. They talked to the blind man and he pointed to where the caramel popcorn boxes were.

The police came over to me, "Miss, where is your mother?"

By then, I had peed on myself and it was running down my legs. I told them, "Outside."

They went outside to the sidewalk to look for her. She was nowhere in sight. I told them, "I am watching her groceries for her." They tried to get me to stop crying. We waited for a little while and she finally came in. They talked to her a few minutes, then they put me and her in the police car.

Mama whispered to me, "Keep your mouth shut." They were in the front of the car and did not hear her.

We went to the courthouse and they put us in a room. A real nice lady came in and asked Mama, "Did you know this child stole some sweets from the blind man's goods?"

"No," she said, "She has never stolen anything in her life."

The lady talked sweet to me saying, "I'm from the Social Welfare."

She said to Mama, "You take her in your care and talk to her about stealing, how wrong it is and how she can go to jail."

That was the reason in the first place why Mama made me stay in the blind man's store because she was afraid I would get caught. I sure got it when I got home. I had welts all over me for a week, just because I got caught.

After the Welfare Lady let us go, Mama got a taxi and the driver helped us load all our bags into the trunk and then we set off to Foggy Creek. She had new things for all us kids.

On Christmas day, we were happy even without our Daddy.

* * *

Mary Judith Messer

One Saturday, Mama told Cheryl, "Judith and I are going to town today. You need to watch out for your brother and sister." She told me, "Hurry up, find your dress, have you got panties on?" and she turned around to look at me. "Get your dress on." I did not want to go, but I dared not say a word. She rushed me, "Hurry up, we will miss the mail wagon."

We walked down to the mail wagon at the mail boxes fast as my bare feet would let me on that old dirt road, with me hoping and praying that we had missed it. But then I would get a beating because I had been too slow finding my dress or walking behind her. We got to the mailboxes just in time. The mailman was turning around.

Mama put me in the mail wagon and got in with me behind his front seat, where his mail was. She made me carry a glass jar in case I got sick on the mountain roads, like I always did. Mama talked to the mailman about Daddy in prison, about all the snakes, and anything else that came into her mind. She could always find something to talk about. Not to me, though, as she never said a word to me on our trip. I did use the jar, though, so I wouldn't get the mail wagon messed up when I got sick to my stomach.

I was so glad when we finally got out on Main Street in Waynesville and my head stopped swimming and my stomach calmed down. We got close to the Court House and all kinds of memories flooded my mind. It was where the nice lady talked with me when I got caught stealing. It was also a nice warm place where we escaped to when we had to run out of the house because Daddy was on a rampage.

We crossed the street and down the sidewalk next to the Court House. There were several little shops there going down the hill. She walked up to one of them and turned the door knob. The door opened and she pulled me in behind her. I looked all around and saw all kinds of things but I had no idea what any of them were. We went in a little and a set of bells rang on the door. An old white-haired lady came over to us. Mama must have known her because she said, "Hello, Aunt Ida, how are you getting along? I thought I would drop in to see you." She was not her Aunt, it's just that

Moonshiner's Daughter

everyone called her that. Mama and her kept talking and I didn't pay any attention because there were so many odd and unusual things in her shop to look at.

"You know, Emily, I have never showed you downstairs, come on," Aunt Ida said, and Mama, who hadn't turned loose of my hand yet, pulled me behind her and followed Aunt Ida. We went one slow step at a time, down into the basement. When we finally reached the last step, it was dark and it made me think of what happened in the school basement. I tried to see in the dark. Aunt Ida hobbled over a few steps and pulled a string that made an old dingy light bulb come on. We could finally see a little better. I strained my eyes to look around. I saw an old rocking chair. *Aunt Ida must live down here,* I thought.

We made our way over to the corner of the basement and Mama started pointing at something. Mama said, "Aunt Ida, what is in that box?" and I began to tremble and shake all over. The last time I saw one of those things, my Papaw in South Carolina was lying in it.

Aunt Ida spoke up real loud and sassy. "That, Emily, is no box! That is my casket. It is specially made just for me, just for me, just my size." She hobbled over to it. If Mama hadn't had hold of my hand in a tight grip, I would have been up those steps and out on the sidewalk in a second. As it was, I stayed put.

"Let me show you what a nice fit," she said. She lifted one leg at a time until she was standing in the middle of it, then she sat down in it and lay down like a pancake. She said, "What a nice fit! You know, Emily, when I get tired upstairs, I just come down here for a nice nap. One day they will dig a deep hole in the cold, dark ground and put my pretty casket down into the hole. What a waste, my nice casket in the ground, with all that dirt on it."

By now, I had wet myself and struggled to get loose, but Mama had me gripped around the wrist like handcuffs. It took Aunt Ida a long time to get out of her casket, but by the time we headed up the steps, I was pulling Mama. I had nightmares about that old woman and her casket for a long time.

Mary Judith Messer

* * *

A week after Christmas, Mama asked Jess if he would take me and her to prison to see Daddy. She left Cheryl with Joanie and Joe. She had no idea how long it would take us, so she didn't know when to tell Cheryl when we would return.

We drove a long way. I was so tired, but I could never go to sleep riding in a car.

"Why don't we stop at a motel and stay the rest of the night and get us some sleep?" asked Jess.

"Okay, fine." Mama answered.

Jess pulled into a motel. He went in and got us a room. We all were very tired and sleepy. Mama put me on a blanket beside the old bed. That old room just had a bed and a small sink. I lay on my blanket. It was dark in the room. You could see a light flashing on and off out the window. There was a sign saying MOTEL VACANCY.

Mama and Jess were in the only bed. I could not go to sleep for the bed was shaking all night. The next morning, we all left the motel and drove the rest of the way to Tallahassee Federal Prison in Florida.

As we got out of the truck, Mama said, "You better not tell your Daddy about me and Jess in the same room."

I sure knew better even before she told me to keep my mouth closed. *I did not want to be dead.*

A lawman brought Daddy into this big room. He had a long chain on his legs and also on his hands. This was the worst way I had ever seen my Daddy look. He had lost some weight but even with the chains on him, he looked real clean in his striped outfit.

He hugged Mama and me and told us he was working in flowers. He had a flower garden.

She told him all about the Lance boys throwing the rocks on the roof and about Papaw dying._ She talked on and on. I said about four words, "I love you Daddy," then before we got out the door, "Please come home." Then we were gone, driving back to North Carolina. We stopped at the same motel, and then we drove on the

Moonshiner's Daughter

next day. I wondered if Mama was worrying about Cheryl, Joe and Joanie. If she was, she sure did not mention it.

We found them all okay, but cold and very hungry. Cheryl was not able to cut any wood by herself. Joe was too small to use a cross cut saw and they had no fire in the dead of winter. The shack was ice. They all had stayed piled up in the bed the whole time.

Mama put Cheryl and me out in the old barn to saw up more logs. I told Cheryl Daddy didn't know when he was going to get out.

* * *

We never had an outhouse at this place, but we had plenty of woods all around the place.

One day Joe was out behind the barn when we heard him scream. Cheryl and I ran to him. He had his overalls down to his feet and next to him was this big copperhead. He was standing real still. Cheryl grabbed a hoe from the barn and made two chops and cut it in two pieces. Joe turned his butt around for us to see if it hit him in the butt. We could not see any holes. I told him, "Next time, put your butt over the creek to shit. The water will wash it away and we will not step in it. Also you can squat down on the log and see any snake." He was very lucky.

He said that the snake struck at him.

Mary Judith Messer

Cheryl Runs Away & We Leave Hell

One day Zeb Lance came down the road. He had this man with him we had never seen before. They come down the bank into the yard.

Zeb said, "Hello!" like nothing had happened. "This is my uncle, Frederick York. He lives over the mountain in Holler Creek."

Frederick said, "Hello."

Cheryl and I were sitting under this big pine tree. We were playing with her doll Patsy.

Mama told us to get our work done before it got dark. We went and got our wood in and the water down. Frederick and Zeb were still on the little porch talking to Mama. She took them in the shack. We heard the record player start up. Her and Zeb were dancing when Cheryl and I got in the shack. They were drinking white lightning. Zeb had a bottle of it in his hands when he came into the yard. We were up most of the night and got very sleepy. Cheryl and I started to bed. Mama told Joe and Joanie to get in her bed. Cheryl and I went on to our bed. Mama came to the door. She had Frederick with her.

Mama said, "Cheryl, Frederick's going to sleep with you." Cheryl made a bad sound like ugh.

Mama said, "What did you say?"

Cheryl said, "I don't want him in here."

"He is sleeping in here anyways, so shut up."

Cheryl never said another word and Frederick was on Cheryl all night, with me laying there next to them.

Zeb was in bed with Mama and the little ones. The next day, Frederick went off with Zeb. Cheryl left me in the yard playing with

Pasty and said she had to go pee. She didn't come back. Mama started calling her; still she didn't come back.

Mama made Joe and me go over to Jim Frank's. They had not seen her. We went down to Florence's and she had not seen her. We went back home. Mama made us go up to the Lance's. "No, we haven't seen her," they said.

We had to go way down below our bus stop to see if the other Lance family down there had seen her. It was real dark when we got home and Mama was walking the floor. She was so mad at Cheryl. If she had found her then, she would have killed her.

All night Mama waited up for her. Days went by; we didn't know where she was. I had no one to help me with the wood and water. I had to do the best I could. I walked all over the woods, and picked up any fallen limbs I could find. I had all the water to carry myself. I sure hoped Cheryl would come back soon. I hoped she had not been killed by a bear or panther. I cried most of the days and when I went to bed, I cried myself to sleep.

Three weeks went by. Jess Welch came by one day and said, "I saw Cheryl."

Mama jumped up, "Where?"

"She was all the way down at this white house. You know where the pavement on the main highway is. She was staying in that house on the right side of the highway. I don't know the people."

"Jess, will you take me to get her?"

He shook his head. "I wouldn't make her come back. She'll only run away again. If she wants to come home, she will." But Mama wouldn't hear no and so Jess took Mama to see her.

Cheryl told us later the people in the white house had taken her in. She was helping care for their small child. They were very good to her, but she was ready to come home.

Mama told her how worried she has been and that we all missed her so much.

She said, "I will go home," and she came back with them. We kids hugged and kissed her and cried. We were so glad to have our oldest sister back. But her stay with us didn't last long, on account of Frederick again.

Mary Judith Messer

* * *

Frederick was over forty years old when he came up to our house and spent the night in Cheryl's and my bed. He had just got out of prison for shooting a man on Holler Creek to death. He had been in prison for twenty years. He killed one man when he was trying to shoot another man. Frederick came back some more and he tried to be very nice to Cheryl every night he was in her bed. Frederick wanted Cheryl to go over the mountain with him to Holler Creek Mountain. His mother and father lived over there and he wanted her to live with him on that mountain on Holler Creek. His Daddy and his Mama were around eighty and she was almost blind. He wanted Cheryl to be with his mother and daddy while he was in the woods making moonshine. Jess Welch' wife and Julie Lance, Ward Lance's wife, were his sisters.

So Mama gave in and had a talk with Cheryl. Cheryl said she would go with Frederick, why, I don't know. *I guess she thought she would do anything to get away from our shack.*

One day soon after that, Mama got a card from Daddy. He wrote that he was getting out on Saturday, a week from then. We all kissed and were very happy. I wondered, though, what he would say about Cheryl going off to Holler Creek Mountain with a man old enough to be her daddy.

Mama was very worried about Daddy coming home. She warned us kids not to tell him about the Lance boys coming down all the time.

Then, the next night, she told Joe and me to go out to the barn, pull Old Pat out of the barn and take a match and set the hay on fire. She didn't want him to see all the logs gone from his barn that she had made us cut up for firewood. She was so afraid he would kill her for us sawing up his log barn.

Joe and I went out to the old log barn. We pulled Old Pat out and tied her lead to the house post that held up the porch. Then we climbed up into the barn loft and Joe struck a match and dropped it into the hay. The fire burned up real high. We jumped out of the

Moonshiner's Daughter

loft and before we got away from the barn, the flames were shooting all over the barn. We heard all the chickens making all kind of noise. We ran to the shack. Flames were reaching the sky. The heat from it was burning our skin and we were on the porch. Old Pat tried to get loose. Mama made us take her around behind the shack. What a sight, red, red, flames going up to the sky. In less than half an hour, our barn was gone up in flames. I will never forget all the snakes that went crawling from that burning barn in all directions. Mama said we better tell Daddy that the Lance boys burned down his barn or he would beat us to death. The next day Mama told me and Joe to go over the mountain to Holler Creek and tell Cheryl that her Daddy was coming home on Saturday.

We went through the woods to the top of the mountain. At the very top, we came to a barb wire fence. We crawled through and walked a good piece down though the woods where we saw a trail and kept walking. We soon saw a main road. The road was a dirt road but it was a lot better than the road in Foggy Creek. We didn't know which way to go out the road to the left or to the right. So we just went left. We walked that road a good ways. We were getting very tired and hungry but we kept walking. We walked around this big turn. Joe said, "Look up on that hill. There is a house." It was the only house we had seen. Not even a barn had we seen. We walked on toward it. We saw this real old man, all bent over, standing in the yard. We called out to him, but he didn't hear us. We called out lots more, when all of a sudden out of that shack walked our sister.

We ran up on the bank but it was too steep. We got down on hands and knees and crawled up that mountain to a house that made our old shack look like a mansion. Cheryl laughed and ran to us and we hugged. The old man was standing, just watching us.

"This is Sam York, Frederick's Daddy," Cheryl said.

We went inside with Cheryl. She let us meet Frederick's mother. Her name was Lonie. She could not see us very good. She also was all humped back.

Cheryl said, "Frederick is up on the park making moonshine. You stay as long as you can."

Mary Judith Messer

We did not want it to get dark on us before we got over that mountain. The old man, Sam, put some eggs in an oatmeal box and gave them to us. That was a good thing, because our chickens all burned up in the fire. Even as steep as that mountain was, they had a little potato patch. They had chickens and a goat.

"Cheryl, do you like living with the old people and Frederick?" I asked.

"Yes, I do."

We hugged her goodbye and slide down the hill. We never knew how that shack sat up on that mountain and never blew off. We were real sorry to leave her up there.

That Saturday, our Daddy made it home from prison. He was with a man he got a ride with. He was in shock to see his barn all burned up. He lost his plow, his sled and all his horse bridles and saddles, all his tools. All he had left was Pat and the halter on her.

Mama said first thing, "Those old Lance boys did it. They set fire to your barn."

He cussed lots, then he got the news that his firstborn child had gone to live with this man over on Holler Creek Mountain. We thought he would hit Mama, but he didn't. He said, "I am going to get the hell out of here. I am going to get the hell out of here with my kids."

We were all standing in the yard when we saw two people come around the turn. They were on horseback. As they got closer, we could make out it was Florence. She was all dressed up. She looked like a cowgirl. She had her man friend with her on the other horse. He also looked like a cowboy. Florence was very pretty. Her and Mama really liked each other. She used to come see Mama a lot, but she had sugar diabetes and had to take shots. Every time we saw her, she looked so nice. She had the prettiest clothes. Mama told her we were leaving as soon as Daddy could find us a house somewhere. She told Mama she was very sorry to see us go, but maybe we'd be better off out of Foggy Creek. Mama had told her about the mean Lance boys. I think she told her everything she knew. I know she told her Daddy beat her a lot.

Florence said, "Goodbye" and rode with her friend out of sight.

Mama couldn't know that Florence would leave out of Foggy Creek before she did.

* * *

A day later, Cheryl came home. When she found out we were moving out of Foggy Creek, she wanted to move with us. All us kids were so happy.

Mama and Daddy sent me and Cheryl to the Rolling Store on Tuesday. A little sprinkle turned into a downpour by the time we got to the Rolling Store. Mr. Honeycut put our groceries in plastic bags instead of paper sacks. As we started back, the rain came down harder and we were soaked to the bone. I saw this bank ahead of us that hung out over the road somewhat. I took a run for it with Cheryl right behind. We got under this big chunk of dirt and grass and we were in the dry. We huddled under that over hang for awhile in hopes the rain would stop. Hail balls started coming down. All of a sudden, the whole bank, all that red dirt, started falling down on us. We ran out from under it and looked up to see Jack Lance standing up there. He had pushed the dirt down on us. We had red clay mud all over us; our hair was such a mess. He was just standing on the hill laughing at us. Our cotton dresses were all covered with mud. We were mad and crying at the same time. We had no choice but to keep going up the road in the pouring rain. When we got to Florence's little shack, we saw two cars there. A man was standing on the porch.

I called to him, "Where is Florence?" We wanted to tell her about Jack pushing down the bank on us.

He said, "Miss Shelly is dead."

We never said another word, just took off running up the road as fast as our wet and dirty bodies could go. As we got close to the shack, we could see Mama out on the little old porch watching for us. The rain had washed most of the mud off of us, which was a good thing. Before we reached the porch and could catch our breath,

Mary Judith Messer

we started shouting "Florence is dead! Florence is dead!" She could not understand a word we were saying. Finally after about five times, she understood. She turned white as a sheet and started to tremble all over. She fell back in this old split bottom chair. She dropped her face to her knees. She was crying like a baby. She finally asked how she died.

We said we didn't know. Later she found out, it was the sugar diabetes. Mama really loved Florence. Two days later, she was told when they would bury Florence but she didn't go to the funeral. While they were having her funeral, Mama made us three kids go down to Florence's little shack. She told us to get some pretty clothing of Florence's to remember her by because she did not need them anymore.

We did as we were told and walked down to her little shack and went in. I thought *it's so quiet without Florence.* We saw the table where Mama sat with her. We saw her old mother's quilt. We three got our arms full of Florence's clothing, while Florence was lying in church in her casket. I never remember what Mama did with Florence's clothing. She never put a rag on. We kids never saw a rag after that day. She must have put them away in this very old trunk that she had and we never got to see into it.

Two days before Daddy got back from Waynesville looking for us a house, Joe was outside playing with these long matches, the same kind we burned down the barn with. Cheryl and I were not paying him much attention when all at once, fire was all over the woods. The fire spread real fast. It went up to the top of the mountain.

All of us just stood around looking at it as it spread up the side of the mountain, nothing we could do. That day Joe with his matches burned over 1200 acres, up to the Park and Cataloochee. Every man around turned up to fight it and they finally put it out.

* * *

Frederick was back over all the time. Some nights he stayed all night. Daddy seemed to like him okay. Daddy finally found us a house in Hazelwood. It was in front of the Hazelwood Prison Camp in the Donald Smith house, just a jump and hop from the Hazelwood School where we went when we lived in Ninevah. It was a very happy day when we left Foggy Creek for good. No more Lances. No more walking almost a mile to the bus. No more snakes, no more being beat up by the Principal. I could have written a hundred pages of no mores, but I was just so happy to get away from that place. I know Mama and all the rest were too, even Daddy wanted out after his barn was all burned down.

The only sad thing about leaving Foggy Creek was having to give up Old Pat. Right before we left, Daddy took her over to the Franks. Jim and Lulu Frank had given us lots of buttermilk and butter and even some things out of their garden like corn, cabbage and other good food while Daddy was in prison. We sure needed it. We were four real HUNGRY KIDS, waiting for our Daddy to get out of prison. Anyway, Mama owed them for all that food, over two years worth, and Daddy couldn't pay them back any other way so he gave them Old Pat. Besides, what would we do with a horse living back in town? Even though I had taken more than one spill off her back, I was sad to have to leave her. Good bye, Old Pat.

And as far as our dog, Old Brownie, he had disappeared during the winter. Just as well, I guess. Most people fed their dogs table scraps and we never, ever had any. I guess he took up with another family who did. Goodbye, Old Brownie, we were all sad he was gone.

Mary Judith Messer

Daddy and his drinking buddy who he married my sister to when she was about fifteen. His buddy was over 40.

Hazelwood, then Hall Top & Mauney Cove

We were now in a very new world. No wood to cut, no snakes, just a new world. The house was pretty nice. It had three bedrooms, a kitchen, a nice living room, and most of all, an inside bathroom.

No more carrying water! Cheryl and I were so very happy. The second day in our new house, Frederick came to the house. He talked to Mama a good while. Cheryl and I did not know what they were talking about; they talked real low and in a little while, Mama came to Cheryl. "Frederick has a taxi outside. You, me and Frederick are going for a ride. Judith, you watch Joe and Joanie till I get back."

The last thing Cheryl got to say as they went out the door was, "Where are we going?"

Mama and Frederick went to the court house and she signed for Cheryl to be married to Frederick. Frederick took Cheryl back to the top of Holler Creek Mountain. She never got to stay but two days in our new place. I was real lonesome without her. Finally, though, Mama got to plug up her washing machine which wasn't new anymore. Rain had blown in on it at the Foggy Creek shack and it had already started to rust out.

It was so very good to live like any other little girl in a nice house with electricity and indoor bathrooms. Joe and I now only had to walk a block to the elementary school. We had such fun. We went up on top of this real high hill and we could look down below at the whole town of Hazelwood. We went exploring around there every chance we got.

We did not stay for long in this nice house. Our landlord, the Smith's, lived nearby. Mrs. Smith worked at the Dayco Plant and she was real nice. She had two boys and her husband, Donald. Mama made us go in their house one day after she saw Donald leave. She told us to get us some of their clothes.

Well, when the Smiths got home and found some things gone, we had to give it all back and move again.

* * *

Now you think that's bad. Daddy moved us on the side of the hill up on Hall Top Road. This was worse than a shack. Old plank floors, bed bugs everywhere. Bed bugs were all over our bodies when we sat on the couch, up our legs, just everywhere. I had to walk this trail around the mountain to carry water and now with Cheryl gone, it was all up to me, the water carrier.

Mary Judith Messer

The toilet outhouse was all the way down this hill below the shack. We sure had a hard life. I just hated the wash days, it was the worse. Carry water up this hill. One day I was walking down the trail, and I stepped on this piece of broken bottle. I cut a big gash in my foot and the blood poured out. I tried to get up to the shack with a blood trail all the way. I got up the trail, but I started to get so weak. Joe screamed for Mama. I lay down on the side of the hill, before I could get to the shack and Mama walked out to the yard. She saw all the blood down the trail, took one look at me and fell over in the yard.

Joe kept screaming and running around. He finally ran up the mountain across this old dusty road. Sally Mae James lived up there. Her mother lived in one house, Sally Mae lived in the other. Joe ran and told her about my foot. Here came Sally Mae running. She had this bottle in one hand and a rag in the other. All the while, Mama was lying all spread out on the ground.

Sally Mae rushed up to me and got the blood stopped. She poured the medicine on the gash and then tried to wake Mama. "Emily! Emily! Get up. You need to take this child to get her foot sewed up. Get up!" Mama finally came to and sat up. My foot had this white rag around it. For a few weeks, I stayed off my foot, but I never got to go to the doctor. It left this big, wide scar on my right foot.

* * *

Daddy now had a firewood and stove wood cutting business. He would cut up huge oak trees, which burned best, and locust and chestnut. He got himself plenty of wood customers. Most of them were colored folks from the other side of town. He only got around fifteen dollars a load and most of the old ladies that bought his wood got checks from the state. They would get his wood on credit. Some went over seventy-five dollars and Daddy stopped bringing them wood at that point. Joe and I had to always help load the wood and then unload it when we got to their houses, on their porches. We got lots of splinters in our fingers and never got a penny helping Daddy. I guess he thought just putting a roof over our head was pay enough.

When the outside was so cold, snow flakes fell through the cracks in the walls, and we were sick all the time with colds and in bed with the flu. Mama still had her washing machine. She had to put it in the very small room we used for the kitchen. Again, it just sat there, no electricity to run it with. She cooked on a wood stove when she had something to cook.

When autos drove up that dusty road, we could not believe all the dust that came off that road into our shack. We were only a few feet from it. We coughed our heads off from all the dust.

We now went back to East Waynesville School. I made sure I didn't drink any water at school so I wouldn't have to go to the bathroom before it was recess time. I did not want to run into that old man by myself. I saw him a lot at school. He was always watching me, walking around with that broom.

Joe and I walked down the old dusty Hall Top road. We had to walk all the way to the bottom of it to catch the bus. Alice Jane Sisk lived on the left side of the road. Where we had to wait on the bus with Alice Jane every morning, she wanted to always start a fight. She had not forgotten the time we almost killed her in that big reservoir with the fire.

One morning we were going at it, I had her by the hair and she had me by the hair. I got her down in the old road and she got me down. All the other kids at the stop including the Parrott's kids were watching us. Joe saw us and was screaming; he picked up a rock and hit her in the back. I still had her by the hair. I got hold of her top and pulled off her top. She had no bra on and she put her hands over her breasts. She was so embarrassed. She took out running into the door of her house. She never had any breasts anyways. Me and Alice Jane never fought any more after that. We tried to let each other be.

* * *

Mary Judith Messer

Not long after, we started seeing black widow spiders crawling around inside the shack. We would stomp them, but it was no use with all those bed bugs and now spiders.

I guess Mama and Daddy finally got sick of the dust and bed bugs and spiders and Daddy moved us about a mile and half around Hall Top Road. This time the house was much better, but we had to carry water downhill from up on top of a hill. Now Joe sometimes helped me. We got some bug spray. Mama sprayed all the bed things and washed the covers. She even sprayed every inch of the couch for the bed bugs. She never wanted to move them with us to the new place. She used five cans of spray. I can never know how many she killed, but we never had them again.

Mama was still drinking. Sometimes it was real bad. One day for no good reason, she got a load of apple tree limbs. She whipped me till blood ran out of my legs. I squatted down in a corner to save my legs and she cut the blood out of my back and arms. I think she beat me on account of Joe. I ran him through the house and hit him. My welts never went away for a long time.

Now we walked around the road to catch the bus to Lake Junaluska school. We walked all the way to Mauney Cove Road. We caught the bus at the mail boxes in Mauney Cove. Lake Junaluska School was okay except for Joe's teacher. Mama had to go down and get onto the teachers three times. One of Joe teachers just hated him. She beat him very bad one time. He was blue all over his butt, his hips and legs. It never did us much good for Mama to go down and get onto the teachers. They got meaner to us kids. Now Joanie was in school and walked with us. I don't think any mean things happened to her at school.

Daddy started making his moonshine again. He stayed drunk all the time. We lived there on the top of Hall Top mountain for three years and never had a garden. The hillside was too rocky. We didn't have any chickens or pigs either, just a new fuzzy dog named Fuzzy.

* * *

Moonshiner's Daughter

Daddy had a chance to buy a real good house about half mile on around the Hall Top Road. The house was more on the Mauney Cove side than Hall Top. When we went to look at the place, we all were overjoyed. We sure liked the place. Buckshot Franklin and his wife were letting Daddy buy it through the Savings & Loan Company. Daddy had also been farming for "Dog" Underwood, so he had good references. He got the place with lots of land. We were very happy and could not believe our luck. After the State Test Farm house, this one was best. It had two bedrooms, a kitchen, a living room, a bathroom and two small porches. We were so lucky to get the place.

First thing, Daddy set himself up some honey bee stands. He said we would get some good honey.

One day I got on this big bicycle and Joe was on in front of me. We started down this old road, just flying. My legs were too short to reach the peddles. We got to going faster and faster. It was all downhill. We ran across Mauney Cove Road into this barb wire fence. We both got cut all over and our clothing was all torn up. We were hurting bad. I begged Joe not to tell Mama. I was so scared. Mama was still drinking a lot. She put on her records and had a Jones girl over dancing with her some times. She sure could dance, but she never drank. Lots more people were with her drunk and fighting or dancing. Joe never told her how we got cut up and skinned. I guess he saved my life for once because if Mama beat me again, I was for sure she would probably kill me.

One day Daddy robbed his honey bee hives. Joe gave me a big piece of the honeycomb and I ate it all. He was laughing his head off and I said, "What is so funny?"

He said, "You ate all the baby bees too!"

You do not eat honeybees. I got sick and vomited. After that, I have never liked honey very much.

After a long time, Frederick brought Cheryl to see us. We were so very happy to see our sister. She looked the same as when we saw her last time. She didn't tell us much about her life. She

Mary Judith Messer

seemed very afraid to talk. She said nothing when Frederick was around.

Frederick and Daddy talked for hours. Frederick drank too so he was a good drinking buddy. Daddy had started taking Joe up in the mountains with him. He made him help with his moonshine and help him pull tan bark off trees to sell. Mama didn't like it one bit that Daddy made him go and work with him (and never gave him a penny). Mama talked about it all day. She told me, "You should have to go and work with him." Some days I did have to go help him.

I was going to school in the snow and ice. I tried to get Daddy to buy me some shoes. I was barefoot and I only had a thin sweater for warmth. He wouldn't even give me five cents for an ice cream.

Along came Joanie. She told Daddy this girl at school had this pretty red coat. She only wanted ten dollars for it. Daddy pulled out his wallet without another word and gave her the ten dollars. She had another coat she had just gotten from the Lions Club. I had gotten too big for them to take me because they took only the lower grades I was told. My feet were frozen numb. It took a half day at school before the feeling came back in them. I was made fun of all the time. Anything Joanie asked him for, she always got. It made me always feel like the black sheep of the family.

One day Joe and I walked through the apple orchard. We went down to Mrs. Kellie Norris's. We liked to stop and see her when we could. She had this real small house next to the creek. We liked Kellie a lot. She had a house full of children, but half them were gone in the Army and others were married and gone. One day this boy came to see her. She said, "This is Clifford Jones. He is my nephew."

I was bashful, but I said, "Hello."

Joe and I went on up through the apple orchard. We knew better than to stay gone long. The next day Daddy was drunk and sitting on the couch. We got a knock on the door. I opened the door and who was on our porch but Clifford Jones.

Daddy said, "Come on in Clifford. Come in. What do you want?"

Clifford said, "I would like to see Judith."

Daddy didn't say a word. I was standing in the doorway that went into the kitchen. I just watched. Daddy's face was red as blood and was getting redder by the minute.

Clifford took out a cigarette, put it in his lips and said, "Terry, you got a match?"

Daddy reached into his pocket and pulled out a pocket knife. He said, "Hell, yes, I got a light." Before you could blink your eyes he had the knife open and was after Clifford who ran out the door. He jumped off that real high porch, then jumped over the road and over the barb wire fence. He was gone in a flash. Daddy shut his knife and put it back in his overalls and reached for his jar of moonshine. That was one day I was afraid for the life of Clifford Jones. His sister was the Jones girl that Mama had up dancing all the time. Her name was Bernice Jones. They moved over on the other side of the mountain from us. Bernice, Clifford and her father only, there was no mother.

One day, Mama, Daddy and Uncle Paul were all drinking. They were going to Hazelwood for two days and told me to stay and watch over the house. They took Joe and Joanie with them. I was all alone when Bernice Jones dropped in. She said, "Hey. Where is everyone?"

I said, "Mama, Daddy, Joe and Joanie all went off with Uncle Paul and his friends to have a party at his friend's house in Hazelwood."

"Why didn't you go?"

"Mama made me stay here and watch the house."

We talked for a while. Bernice was a little older than me. Boy could she dance. She buck danced so good. Wallace Jones, her Daddy, and Clifford both liked to play the guitar. Some more of those Jones boys were Terry, Charles and I don't remember the others, but Terry was not living at home. Charles was in the service.

Mary Judith Messer

Bernice said, "Gosh. I came up to listen to your Mama's records and dance." Now the Joness were real poor people. They didn't have records. They lived in shacks like we did.

"Bernice, I would never dare fool with Mama's record player or records." That was one thing you sure didn't do.

So Bernice and I just sat and talked on the porch. We talked about girl talk. We did not talk about boys. She and I were not interested in boys at all. By this time it was getting late.

"I better start walking because it's getting late," Bernice said. She had to walk all the way to Ninevah.

"Bernice," I said, "I am so afraid to stay by myself when it gets dark. Can you please stay all night with me?"

"I would like to, but I have no way to call and ask Daddy."

We Longs were up in the world. We had gotten us a phone, of all people with a phone, the Longs! I tried to get Bernice to call someone over where she lived so they could go to Bernice's shack and ask her Daddy, but she could not think of anyone with a phone. They had only lived in the place for a week.

I pleaded with her to stay. Always before when we were left alone, we had Cheryl. We were always scared to death, but we did have each other to be with.

"Judith, I know what. You can come with me and stay with me tonight. Did you not say your Mama and Daddy won't be back for two days?"

"Yes, but I was told not to leave this house. Daddy will be very mad if he finds out I have left."

"But he won't find out. At daylight in the morning, you can walk back home."

We talked about it for more than thirty minutes. I was so afraid.

"Have you eaten? Daddy has cooked supper and I am sure he won't care if you come to supper and stay with me tonight."

"I have nothing to eat."

"Okay, then come on," she urged.

"Let me lock the doors."

Moonshiner's Daughter

We started walking around Hall Top Road. I looked back at the house. I stopped. "No," I said to Bernice. "I am afraid to leave the house."

"Come on now. It won't be long till dark. I got to get home."

"I better go back," I stammered, and turned for home.

Bernice said, "I guess you ain't afraid to stay alone in the dark."

That did it. I started walking with her real fast. We got to her place just before dark. Her Daddy, Wallace, was setting a bowl of soup beans on the table. I did not see Clifford anywhere. Her place was very small and Clifford's bed was over in the other corner. A table and cook stove was in the middle of the room. Wallace invited me to sit down and let me break off a piece of corn bread. I was very hungry so the beans and corn bread were very good.

"Daddy, can Judith spend the night with me?" Bernice asked.

"Why, sure. Does Terry and Emily know where you're at?"

I looked at Bernice. She said, "Yes, they know. They said she could come."

"Fine, then stay," her Daddy said.

Bernice and I lay in bed and talked and giggled half the night. She had bed bugs. We scratched also all night. Sometime in the night, I heard the door open. It must have been Clifford, I thought. I went to sleep right at daylight. I heard this loud knock on the wood door. It woke me fast. Bernice was also awake.

Someone went to the door. Suddenly my bed was shaking. I looked up to see Clifford with his foot on the mattress shaking the bed with his foot.

He finally said what he wanted after Bernice blessed him out for waking us up.

"Judith. You are in big trouble. Your Mama called the lady that lives in a trailer up the hill and said you better get home and fast!" I hit the floor. *How did she know I was over here? How did she know this woman had a phone? How come they are home so soon? How...? How...? How?"*

Mary Judith Messer

I was crying so bad. Bernice and I had slept with our dresses on so I just ran out the door. I never ever told Bernice good bye. I was now afraid for my life. I hurried all the way, fast as I could. When I got to Mauney Cove, I stopped at the Sherrill's house. I don't know why I didn't go back Hall Top Way. A lot shorter, I guess. I knew no one on Hall Top Road had a phone and I needed to talk to Mama bad. The Sherrill's let me use the phone. Mama was as mad as she could be. She said, "Your Daddy is gonna kill you."

I was crying so bad, I couldn't hardly hear what she was saying. She told me to "get the hell home."

I stayed at the Sherrill's for about an hour. I called Mama again. She said, "Judith, if you do not get home at once, your Daddy will beat you to death."

I kept crying but thanked the Sherrill's and started real slow up Mauney Cove Road. I got about half a mile from the house and I stopped in at a Palmer man's house. I asked to use the phone.

Mama came on the line. She said, "Judith, your Daddy has cut some of the biggest limbs off the cherry tree. I went out and got some smaller ones for him to whip you with. He is asleep and very drunk. Maybe he will sleep off the drunkenness and not beat you so much. Just get here before he wakes up or you will be dead."

I walked to the house thinking *"I won't be alive tomorrow"* then I walked into the yard where Joanie and Joe were playing out back of the house.

Mama came on the porch. She said, "Little girl, you better be thankful I threw away those other limbs he had. He would have killed you with them."

I looked in the house and saw some long limbs. I was crying so hard, begging her to help. In my heart I knew she couldn't help me. Even when Mama whipped us, she was very bad. She would cut the blood out of me, but Daddy almost killed me when he beat me.

He was still in bed. I stayed outside so I wouldn't wake him up. As long as he was asleep, I wouldn't get killed. I got to live. He slept for over an hour after I got home.

But then I heard him rustle and he called me from inside the house. He shouted, "That G.. damn Jones boy you were with…".

Moonshiner's Daughter

Before I could tell him anything, he drug me up the steps into the house. I have never had such a beating in my life. I knew for sure, I would die.

Mama stood there, ringing her hands, and begged him to stop. When he broke up all the limbs on me, he grabbed a stick of stove wood. I fainted out only to come back with him still beating me.

When I woke up again, Mama was putting water on my head. She laid me in bed and that's where I stayed for a few weeks, only getting up to use the bathroom. Mama tried to get me to eat, but I couldn't hold anything down. I got so weak, I just wanted to die.

Mama told me later that they had come home early that day because Paul and everyone was drunk and fighting, so she and Daddy just came home early.

That beating I took, because I was too scared to be left alone for two days, will live with me all the rest of my life. I will never know how I pulled out of it and back to life. I was near death for weeks. *Spare the rod and spoil the child...maybe it should be spare the child and spoil the rod.*

Mary Judith Messer

Daddy Goes Back To Prison & I Escape

Daddy got caught with his still again. The revenuers got him. He was tried and sent off to Tallahassee, Florida, to the Federal Pen there.

We all went up on the top of Holler Creek Mountain to see our sister, Cheryl. We had to walk most the way up the mountain.

Mama saw Cheryl before we got up the hill. She was out in the yard. Mama said, "She is pregnant." We hugged her and Mama asked her, "Are you going to have a baby?"

She said, "No, I don't think so. I'm maybe just getting fat."

We looked at her. She was only fat in her belly. She said she had to take care of both the old people because Frederick was back in the mountains all the time. We never knew it then, but Frederick had come close to killing another man. He shot him in the shoulder for stealing a jar of moonshine.

We sure were glad to see our Cheryl.

She asked me, "Why are you black and blue all over?" It had been a long time since I got the beating from Daddy and I still was black and blue. I had not been back to school because I was too ashamed of the lingering marks.

Mama made Frederick promise us that he would drive Cheryl up to see us more often when he came down out of the woods.

* * *

After only a few months of being gone, Daddy came back home. He had gotten off early for good behavior. He went back to work for Dog Underwood. Frederick came up to see him and he and Daddy started up making moonshine together. One day, they killed this big black bear. On the bus, I told everyone. They made fun of me. The big high school girls pulled my hair and called me, "Black Bear, Black Bear." Everyone on the bus made fun. This Smith girl was real bad to tease me. Frederick and Daddy were running off white lightning, when the revenuers run in on them. They caught Daddy but not Frederick. It was Friday the 13th. Mama had told Daddy, "You should not go to your still today. It is Friday the 13th."

He was again sent to the Federal Pen in Tallahassee, Florida. This time it was for six months. He would not tell them who was with him at the still or who his partner was. So Frederick got out of it. He never had to do no time.

* * *

Soon, my life took a turn for the better. We had a regular visitor that I had known a long time, a small, dapper man named Sam Queen, Sr. who always came up to whatever house we lived in. He always took Mama and Daddy to vote. He paid them two dollars each to vote for the Democrats because all the Queens were Democrats.

He called the square dances for locals and tourists at the Maggie Playhouse. He had even taken a dance team to Washington, D. C. to dance for President and Mrs. Roosevelt and the King and Queen of England in 1939. He told me to call him "Grandfather." I was glad to for I liked that old man. Mama and Daddy liked him also. They let him take me to the Maggie Playhouse to watch him call the dances. He sure could square dance.

Around the time I was thirteen years old, Grandfather Queen had me to come down to his little motor court at the end of Mauney Cove Road and help his wife Glee in the house. I was crazy about her, too. She was so good to me and was the head of the Department of Social Services. She even gave me money for the little jobs I did for her and then Grandfather would drive me back home. He never made me walk.

One day, after Grandfather Queen brought me back home, he told Mama that Lois Queen, his son's wife, needed some help taking care of her children while she ran their tourist ranch called

Mary Judith Messer

Queen's Farm and Dude Ranch, on Dellwood Road. Now I knew all about Lois and Grandfather's son, Richard Queen. Grandfather had already taken me by the farm a lot. Lois had all these guest rooms she rented out to visitors, mainly from Florida. The guests also got to eat in the dining room. She had fresh vegetables right out of their garden that her help grew for her. All she did was go and gather the vegetables and her cook made the best meals for the guests.

I really loved Queen's Farm from the first time I saw it. So when Grandfather asked Mama could I go over to the farm and help Lois for the summer and get paid, I thought I must be dreaming.

"Mama, please, please, can I go?" I begged.

She said, "I'll have to ask your Daddy."

By now he was out of the pen again. He let me go. One less mouth to feed, I reckon.

When I got over to the farm, Lois gave me my own room, and I did not want to go back home ever again. I just wanted to stay there forever.

A Mother's Helper &
Paying the Mortgage

You know by now my story of how my life growing up in the mountains of Western North Carolina was. My life changed with me over at the Queen's Farm with Lois and Richard Queen and their young children. My job was to watch after them so they wouldn't get hurt or anything. I guess you could say I was a mother's helper.

The oldest was a boy, Jimmy. Next was a very pretty little girl with puffy cheeks. Her name was Sara Margaret and she was named after her Aunt Sara, Richard's sister. Next was a girl, Susan, who was badly crippled by cerebral palsy. She had braces on her legs. Grandfather kept her most of the time during the summer. Then came Frank Graham who was named after one of Richard's employers, Senator Frank Graham. Then came George Pryor, the baby at that time, named after Congressman George Shuford, who Richard had worked for. Sam Love, the youngest, came later and was named after Grandfather Queen.

On the farm was a big horse barn and riding stable. The hired help took the guests of the farm on trail rides and pack trips on the horses. I got anything I wanted to eat. Sara slept with me lots in my room, even though there was plenty of room in the real big white house. Miss Smith kept the motel rooms clean and lots of others helped cooked. We also had our own dish washer. It was real fun to stay with the Queens. I never had it so good.

One day a taxi drove up around to the back of the main house, where the kitchen was and right next to where my bedroom was. Lois saw the taxi and went out to see who it was. I walked out of my room, right in front of the taxi. Mama and some woman were in the taxi. Mama said, "Lois, I need to talk to Judith."

I walked over to the car. Mama was very drunk but managed to say, "Judith, your Daddy has sent me after you. He wants you home now."

Right away I started crying. "Mama, please don't make me go back."

Lois stuck her head in the window of the car. She talked low to Mama. "Emily, you don't want to make Judith go back, do you?"

Mama started talking about money to Lois. Lois tried to tell her how good I was doing, that I had good food and a room of my own, but Mama didn't hear what she said.

Mama said, "Terry is months behind on his house payments and is going to lose our place if I can't find some way to help him."

Lois then turned to me, 'Judith, how much money do you have saved up?" I told her that I would go and count it. I counted all my money. I only got $15.00 a week pay but if I did anything for the Guests, they gave me tips. I came out of my room. "Lois, I have one hundred and seventy five dollars counting all my change."

Lois told Mama, "Judith has all the back house payments except for seventy five dollars and I will give her the seventy five and she can pay me back." We gave Mama all the money she needed and she let me stay. The taxi slowly backed down the driveway and Mama and her friend were gone. I cried some more just from sheer relief I wouldn't have to leave.

The kids and I had so much fun that summer. Sometimes Sam, Jr. would bring his kids over to play, too. He was Richard's brother. His wife's name was Mary. They were school teachers. Rachel was the oldest, Sara's age, and Joe Sam was the boy, around Frank's age. We all had fun in the playground in front of Queen's Farm. We had swings, slides and everything. We even had a sand box for George. Best of all was when Grandfather came and set each of us, one at a time, in the saddle on one of the horses. I was never afraid to ride there because he always held onto the bridle. He gave us all our turn at riding. He led us up to the stables at the horse barn and back. We had such fun.

"Grandfather" Queen holding Sara and her cousin Joe Sam on a horse. Next was my turn!

We loaded up in the car one time and all went to see Lois's mother, Mrs. Pryor, in Bat Cave. She and her husband had the biggest table, having raised twelve children of their own, and it was full of the best food you ever ate. I was told to call her Grandmother Pryor, like all the other kids.

Susan, the little girl who had cerebral palsy, was put in a crippled children's home where they could give her physical therapy. She had scars on her legs and arms from many operations. She never got to come over to Grandma Pryor's house that summer. She was in Asheville.

When she was home for Christmas or some holiday, I had a very hard time with her. I had to carry her to the bathroom. Those old braces on her legs were very heavy and made of steel. They hooked in her shoes. I had to take the braces loose to pull down her little panties. Sometimes I was too slow and she had an accident and

Mary Judith Messer

Lois would scold her real bad for waiting so long to tell us she needed to go to the bathroom. Then I would have to take the braces all the way off to clean her and put on more clean panties.

Little Susan couldn't hold up her head. She laid it on her shoulder like her neck wouldn't hold her heavy head up. She didn't use her hands much either so we had to feed her most times.

Sometimes the other kids took away her toys and playthings and she would let out a squall. If Lois heard her, Susan got scolded. "Now Susan, stop that! No more of that!" She never made the kids give the toy back. But that was no different than how she treated her other children. I realize now that Lois wanted Susan to learn the same lessons. She wanted them to learn to take up for themselves, which they all learned to do, including Susan. It still made me feel bad, even so.

Jimmy was the oldest. Jimmy was just in the second grade, but he could read anything, almost better than me. He could pick up most any book and know what all the words meant.

Well, Lois was a school teacher the rest of the year when she wasn't running the Farm. Richard was George A Shuford's Congressional Administrator in Washington, D.C. Richard stayed in Washington a lot; he was gone up there half the time. Lois pretty much ran the farm by herself in the summer with all her help. Grandfather came by the farm every Saturday night on his way to the Maggie Valley Playhouse. He stopped and asked Lois if it was okay to take me with him to watch him dance and call the square dancing. She let me go every time he came and asked.

I just loved that banjo and fiddle playing. The best music in the world was old country square dancing music. Grandfather with his red suspenders was out on the dance floor calling "Swing your partners", and "doe-se-doe." The women dancers on his team had all the checkered dresses on with the red checks and white. You could see all the big petticoats under the dresses. They looked beautiful.

The men had red checkered shirts and all had red suspenders like Grandfather's. He always wore some tan colored pants that he fastened his suspenders to. I could hardly wait till Saturday night to get to go.

One night someone came to the front door where the lobby was and rang the door bell.

Lois answered the door, thinking it was a tourist looking to rent a room. But she came to find me instead. I was watching the children. She said, "Judith. There is a young man at the front door who wants to talk to you. He said his name is Clifford Jones. Do you want to talk to him?

I told her, "No. Tell him I do not want to see him."

Lois went back to the lobby and told him what I said. She said he just walked back down the steps.

About a week after this, Mama showed back up, in a taxi again with this same woman.   Lois was somewhere in the den room with one of her guests. It had been over six months since I had seen Mama from the last time, even though she lived less than two miles away. Again I could tell she was drinking but not as drunk as the last time she came over. She again started this thing, "Daddy wants you home." She said, "You know Clifford Jones came to see you and Lois would not let you see him. He said as long as you stay with the Queens, he don't want to see you"

"Mama," I said, "I know he came over here. I told Lois I want nothing to do with him. I don't even like him. I have never liked him."

She said, "Well, well. You are getting pretty brave, are you? You just go and get your things. Your Daddy wants you home now."

Frank ran to find his mother. I was crying. Lois came out and Frank was running right behind her. Lois saw me crying. She put her arm around me. "Now, now, Emily what is this all about? What's going on anyway?"

Mama stuck her head out the car window. "I have come to get Judith. Her Daddy will be very mad if I do not bring her back. Now, Judith, go get your things."

Lois and Mama kept talking and soon we knew why she had come over again.   Daddy was over two hundred and fifty dollars

Mary Judith Messer

behind what he owed to the Savings and Loan Company and they were going to take his place.

Lois asked me, "How much do you have?"

I knew I didn't have that much money. It had only been six months since I had given Mama every penny I had saved up before. Since it had been the off-season, I knew I hadn't made too many tips and Lois had held back the seventy five dollars I owed her from the last time. I ran to my room once again to count up every penny of money I had to my name. All I could come up with was two hundred and sixteen dollars. So Lois put in the rest of the money. I could work it out with her.

In a repeat from months before, Lois handed over all the money to Mama. She said, "Judith can work out what she borrowed from me."

Mama looked happy and the taxi once again backed down the driveway.

Lois Pryor Queen and J. Richard Queen, Sr. who showed me so much kindness and helped me escape my abusive past.

Moonshiner's Daughter

Helping With The Kids & A New Mother

Everything I could do for our guests, I did, including carrying heavy luggage to the rooms or out of the rooms for tips. I went to the drink machine and got them drinks, or to the freezers where there were big tubs of every kind of ice cream they make where I dipped out some ice cream for their kids, anything just to get my tip.

Before too long, I gave Lois back her money, paid in full. It was little enough to do to scrape and save for a while to keep me from having to go back to the nightmare I had left behind.

* * *

Every day Jimmy, the oldest boy, looked in all kinds of magazines and he ordered all kinds of things out of them, toy soldiers, tanks, you name it. Only in third grade now, he filled out his order blanks his self and got lots of things in the mail every single day. We had fun waiting for the mail every day. We would watch for the mailman to stop at the mailbox down at the road, then run down the hill and bring the mail up to Lois each morning, minus Jimmy's packages, of course.

Jimmy and I liked to tease Sara. She was always walking around like she was some movie star. She prissed around like she was an "it." Jimmy and I teased her and she would run tell her mother.

Lois would come find us. "Now, now, Jimmy and Judith. Stop teasing Sara. Leave her alone." Then she went back to taking care of the guests. Sara was just pretending then, but one day she would go to Los Angeles and become an actress in movies and TV.

She was cute as she could be, and I loved her. Jimmy was just a head higher than she was. She was so fancy.

The younger children were just all around playing one day in front of my room just off the back porch kitchen. Paul, one of the horsemen who worked at the riding stables, was outside changing the oil in one of the farm tractors. He had this big round rubber tub he slid under the tractor motor that he drained the old oil into. He drove off and left that tub full of used black oil just sitting beside the driveway. I think he was going to come back for it.

I was in the kitchen when I heard the baby, George, screaming his little head off. I ran through the other outside porch kitchen where the dish washing man was and the long ice cream and meat coolers were. I was trying to hear where the screaming was coming from. With all the pots and pans clanging from the dishwasher making noise, I thought he was in the dining room. I ran into the dining room, and it was full of guests who were having a meal. I couldn't hear anybody crying in there and I ran back through the long room past the dish washer. He stopped and must have thought I had gone crazy. Then I heard George again, the screaming coming from the back yard. I flew through the screen door as fast as I could go. I saw him. He was standing up in that pan of used oil. He looked like a little black baby. His diaper was black. You could only see his mouth and eyes.

"My, my, what a mess." I said, seeing that little boy as I tried to pick him up. He was slick as glass and I couldn't get a hold of him.

Lois came flying out the door. She tried to calm him down and I ran and got a towel so we could pick him up. He was still screaming like he was dying. When I got back with the towel, I carried him to the bathroom and Lois ran some good, warm water and put bubble bath in the water. We had a bathroom for every bedroom in the big white house so there were plenty of them for us all.

Moonshiner's Daughter

We had to run three bathtubs full of water to get him clean. After that, Lois put me to drying George off. Then she sent someone for Paul. She sure gave him a piece of her mind. We could hear her outside. She was so mad. I will never forget that little black boy. He was such a sweet little boy.

I was growing taller and had put on weight with all that good food and anytime I wanted ice cream, I got it. Lois also was a very good cook. When the cook was out, she cooked herself.

Queen's Farm and Dude Ranch, where I felt
safe and cared about—and made good tips!

After about a year and a half of living at Queen's Farm, at the end of summer, Lois told us kids we were moving up to northern Virginia, right outside of Washington, DC. She said, "Richard has gotten us a house in Alexandria, Virginia. He is coming down to move us up there."

I asked, "Can I go too?"

Mary Judith Messer

"I sure hope so," Lois said. "I need you to watch the children because I'll be teaching school. I hope Emily and Terry let you go."

Richard got back from Washington. He said, "We will leave in three days."

The next day, Lois left Mrs. Smith, her housekeeper, with the children and she took me to Mama and Daddy's house. We drove up to the Hall Top house, parked the car and walked up to the porch and we could hear a drunken party that was going on inside. I was afraid to walk in the door, so Lois walked up the steps.

Mama saw her and walked out on the porch.

Lois tried to talk to Mama, but with all the loud music, Mama could not hear what Lois was saying. They walked out in the yard.

Lois asked, "Can Judith go to Virginia with our family?"

Mama walked out behind the house where Daddy was chopping wood to ask him. After a minute, Lois walked back there too. When Daddy saw Lois, he said, "I guess it'll be okay."

Mama told me, "Judith, you need to stay overnight. We are going up on Holler Creek Mountain to see Cheryl and you need to see her before you go."

Lois said, "That's fine, Judith. When you get back, call me and I will come for you."

I guess Daddy figured that me living with Lois had been good, at least he still had a house to live in on account of Lois and me.

We went the next day to see Cheryl and sure enough, she was going to have a baby. We were all very happy to see each other again. I thought she had changed a lot. She looked all grown up. Her belly was big. She never talked about the baby at all. We all kissed and hugged goodbye. Frederick said he would come with Cheryl more often to see Mama. He had not come with Cheryl to see Mama in a long while.

Mama kept her word to Lois. As soon as I got back, I called Lois and she said she was on the way to pick me up. I told Mama and all the rest, "Goodbye. I will write." I left without any kind of hug.

Moonshiner's Daughter

* * *

At the Queen's, we began rushing to get ready for the long trip. One moving truck was loading up. Then another one came right behind it, and then another. Hardly any stuff being loaded belonged to me 'cause I never had too many things of my own. Most of my clothes Lois had given me from her hand-me-downs. They were somewhat big on me, but I never made a fuss. I was just happy to have some clothing to wear at all. I packed up all I had in a small bag.

The next day, we all started out on the road, two cars of us. The movers were long gone on their way to Alexandria. It was such a long trip, with two cars, and four restless children plus me, Richard stopped half way there and put us all in this real nice motel for us to sleep for the night. We also ate two times, supper and breakfast. Then we were on the way again.

I remembered Grandfather Queen's words to me when I said goodbye. "Judith, you will take good care of the children, won't you?"

I said, "I promise."

I watched him until we were out of sight My new mother was Lois Queen. Since the first day I went to Queen's Farm, I knew she was more a mother to me than my real mother. At least, Lois never tried to kill me. In all the years I was with her, she had never once even hit me.

Mary Judith Messer

Life In Virginia & A Visit From the Feds

We got to our new home in Virginia just about dark. The movers had already set the house full of furniture inside. They were finishing up when we drove up. It was called Warwick Village.

I really liked the place. It had a nice big living room with a T.V. and a kitchen, plus three bedrooms upstairs where we all slept and a large basement with a concrete floor. It was connected on to lots of other apartments, all made of brick in a big circle.

In back, Richard put his charcoal grill. He loved to cook juicy steaks all the time. I never cared for steaks much, but he also cooked hamburgers. That Jimmy just loved steaks. He would eat two whole pieces a meal. We always had French fries all the children loved.

Richard worked for a Congressman in Washington, DC. Lois taught school in Alexandria. Jimmy was in school. Sara, George and Frank were home with me. Susan was left in North Carolina with Grandfather. She just got to come up for special holidays like Christmas. When she was up, it was hard on me. I had to lug her up those stairs to the bed and bathroom. There was only one bathroom and it was upstairs.

Lois had told Mama and Daddy, if they let me go with them to Virginia, she would be sure I got my schooling. Lois was a school teacher as I said before but I never went back to school after I left home. Lois did not home school me either. I stayed at home and took care of all the children. I left school after the eighth grade. I did not care.

I was with good people. Lois was more a Mama to me than my real Mama ever was. After dinner every night, when Lois and

Richard were home, I would walk around the neighborhood and explore. Richard gave all of us money for the movie, popcorn and candy. We walked through the woods a short distance to the theater. Only Jimmy, Sara, Frank and I were able to go. George was too little.

On Armed Forces Day, Richard took us to see the planes and helicopters do the square dance in the air. It was so much fun. I had never hardly been out of the Smoky Mountains before let alone gotten to see movies and planes, helicopters and all.

One Saturday he took us to Washington to see a movie called *Moby Dick*. It was 3D and the movie screen was as big as the whole wall. The big whale looked so real, we thought it would jump out on us. We could just feel all that water splashing. The kids got scared. I had to hold Frank in my lap. We had such a great time. I dreamt about it every night for a long time.

The only other time I had been to the movie was when I was in second grade and the teacher took us to see *Song of the South*. I'll never forget the main character who was Uncle Remus and him singing "Zippy-Dee-Do-Dah, Zippy-Dee-Day" with birds flying around him. I wasn't going to be able to go because I didn't have a nickel to pay my way, but my teacher paid it for me and several other kids so the whole class could go.

* * *

All the time, I saved all the money I could, every penny. Richard gave me a handful of his change every once in a while. I liked the dimes the most. They did not take up much room. I filled my jar full of dimes.

One Saturday, Richard drove us into Washington. He took us to the Capitol to see where he worked in his office. We liked his big black leather chair. We each got to sit in it and turn around. Jimmy wanted to sit in it the most. We fussed with him to give us a turn.

The office was real nice. We got to meet a few Congressmen; most of them had gone home for the weekend, only a few were left to catch up on their work. We went all over the Capitol where we

Mary Judith Messer

saw real big rooms with lots of red seats and they were the hardest we ever sat on. We ran all over the whole place.

We went back to North Carolina for the summer while Congress was having a recess and I went over to see Mama. We all went up on the mountain to see Cheryl again. She had her baby, a little baby boy. She called him Bobbie Lee. He was so cute and sweet.

Cheryl had just had the baby a few days before and Mama got real mad. She said, "That damn Frederick is in there on top of Cheryl having sex and she just got back from the hospital two hours ago."

She could see them through the cracks in the wall. He never let us come in to say hello. We just saw the old people and the baby and we left.

I went back to Lois's. She had a very busy time looking after all those guests and all. Mrs. Smith made sure to make up all the beds with clean linen and kept the rooms clean. She was a hard worker for Lois. She got good tips.

I wished I could help more and get more tips. Grandfather Queen was still calling the square dancing in Maggie. Sometimes I still went with him.

That January, when Congress was called back into session, we all went back to Alexandria. We could see all the lights of Washington from Sara's and my room shining on the water called the Potomac River. They were so pretty. Lois had her sixth child, Sam Love, in November.

I got one letter from Mama the whole time I was in Washington. She needed three hundred and eighty six dollars for house payments. I went and cashed in all my change and Lois got me a money order with all my money. I still lacked thirty-eight dollars. Richard gave it to me. Lois said she made the money order to the Savings and Loan, so Mama and Daddy would not drink up the money even though Mama told me she had stopped drinking.

I sure hated to cash in my dimes. I had two jars full. I loved my little dimes, but that was okay. I started saving again. It took a long time to save.

We all went to church with Lois's people. It was fun to go and hear about Jesus.

I sure liked it up there in Virginia. The lights shining over the water from the Capitol were so pretty.

Jimmy got me to order things. Also he was still ordering all kinds of things. His room was just full of goodies. He got his money orders and mailed two or three money orders a week. He gave me these envelopes to use and we didn't even have to put stamps on them. We watched T.V. and ordered the things they advertised on the Saturday morning cartoon shows. We also ordered things on the cereal boxes. I got a bunch of stars' pictures. They had put their names on them. I loved to get all kind of pictures, signed and all. Jimmy and I were good buddies. If he saw something he thought I wanted, he would write down the address and I would order it. We always got along great, but he was at school all day. The others were with me all day.

One morning, I was cooking breakfast. Lois had shown me how to fix soup and sandwiches for the kids' lunch. She also showed me how to cook eggs and bacon or sausage. Most of the time the children just wanted cereal. I fixed them cereal. Jimmy fixed his own cereal. I was in the kitchen. I had some bacon frying in a pan. Lois and Richard were upstairs getting dressed to go to work.

All at once, I heard George, the toddler. He was just screaming. I ran to the living room and saw him at the bottom of the stairs. He was screaming his eyes out. I picked him up to see if he was hurt. Lois called to me from upstairs. She had been in the shower. She said, "Bring him to me, Judith."

I ran up the stairs. He only had a little bump, on his head. About that time Jimmy called out, "There's smoke coming out of the kitchen!" He was in the living room watching T.V. and eating his cereal.

I ran to the kitchen and the pan of grease and bacon was on fire. Without thinking, I grabbed the hot pan of grease and threw it

Mary Judith Messer

into the sink and turned on the water. I burned my hand good. The black smoke was all over in the kitchen and going down the hall into the living room. Lois had run down the stairs into the kitchen. "Judith are you okay? Are you burned?" She could not see me for the black smoke.

I called out to her and she said, "Come here now. Get out of that smoke."

I was afraid I had set the place on fire. She put salve on my hands and said, "Do not ever again pick up a hot pan like that. You could have caught on fire! And do not put water on hot grease."

She was happy to see I was okay, but her kitchen was not okay. It was smoked black. All the nice kitchen cabinets were so black you could not even tell how they used to look. On Saturday, Lois herself spent all day long scrubbing the kitchen clean. What a mess it was.

Frank, Jimmy, Sara and I had us roller skates. We older kids went down stairs to the cement floor where we had such a good time skating.

The Queen children, on one of my summer visits after I had moved to NY. L. to r. Jimmy, Sara, George, and Frank with baby Sam in the front. Susan was not there.

One evening, Lois and Richard were getting dressed for a night out. There was a knock on the door and I ran to open it.

Two men in dress clothing were at the door. One of them said, "Young lady, who is the man of the house?"

I said, "That would be Richard Queen."

They said, "Tell him to come to the door if he is home."

I said, "Okay."

I ran up the stairs. "Richard, some men want you at the door."

Richard came down to the door. "I am Richard Queen. What can I do for you? Come in, please."

Now they were all standing in the small hallway. One man said, "Do you have a Miss Judith Long living at this address?"

"Why, yes. That was Miss Long that opened the door. What's going on? Is something wrong? She lives with us. She came from North Carolina with us and is one of my family."

All this time, I was standing in the living room and could hear everything that was being said. I was scared. *What kind of trouble am I in?*

One man said, "Mr. Queen, we are with the government. The United States Post Office Department. We are investigating some letters that came from Miss Long. The envelopes had the U.S. Government Stamps on them. We don't believe she was authorized to use the government envelopes."

Richard called to me and I went into the hall where they were standing. "Judith, have you used any of my envelopes? These men are from the U.S. Government. They are saying some government envelopes were mailed with your name on them."

Before I could answer Richard said, "Gentlemen, I also work for the U.S. Government. As I told you, I am Richard Queen. I am George A. Shuford's Congressional Administrator. I work in the Capitol."

"Okay, Mr. Queen" one answered. "I guess the Miss got hold of some of your official envelopes."

I said, "Jimmy and I both have been using the envelopes. I never knew it was against the law."

Mary Judith Messer

One man spoke up, "Well, Miss, it sure is against the law because the U. S. Government paid for that postage."

I could not understand why they had got only my letters and not Jimmy's, too.

Richard said, "Judith, do not ever do that again. I will also talk to Jimmy."

That was one time I was scared of the U. S. Government. I learned a valuable lesson that night.

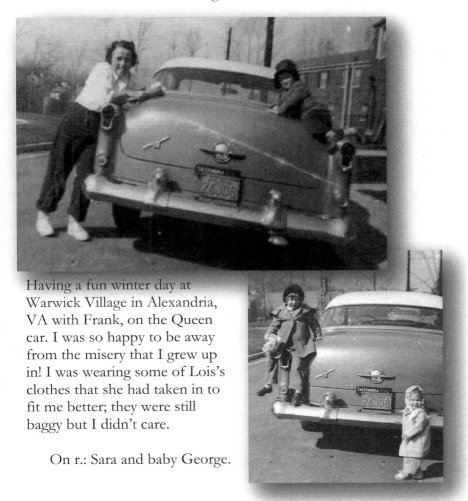

Having a fun winter day at Warwick Village in Alexandria, VA with Frank, on the Queen car. I was so happy to be away from the misery that I grew up in! I was wearing some of Lois's clothes that she had taken in to fit me better; they were still baggy but I didn't care.

On r.: Sara and baby George.

Moonshiner's Daughter

Cheryl Calls & I Move To New York City

Lots of nights, Richard and Lois went out to all kinds of dinner parties. Richard got all dressed up. I will never forget the little mink fur Lois had around her shoulders. It has a real little mink head with a long nose. It also had these little long legs and arms. It was so cute. She wore it every time they had an important luncheon or dinner. I liked to watch her go out the door with that little mink. She had nice dress up things. She gave me all kinds of things to wear.

One night about eight o'clock, Lois called me to the phone. Now I never got a phone call so I was very curious just who could be calling me. It was Cheryl. She was in New York City. She said she had gotten a newspaper when she had gone one day to Mama's house. She had read an advertisement in the paper that said "Come to New York City and make good money working as a maid or housekeeper. We'll send you tickets for bus fare. There's plenty of work in New York City."

She said, "I sent for the bus tickets and here I am. I am now in New York."

I asked, "Where is your baby, Bobbie Lee?"

"I had to leave him on top of Holler Creek Mountain because I was afraid Frederick would find and kill me if I took the baby."

"But, those old people cannot take care of him. They might drop and kill him."

"But, I was so afraid," she said. "I just left Frederick while he was up in them woods making his moonshine."

We talked for a good while then she said, "Why don't you come up here too?"

I said, "I would like to but I have to stay with Lois. She needs me to watch all the children."

My nephew and the elderly in-laws that my older sister had to take care of while her husband was off in the woods moonshining. My sister had to leave her son there when she ran away to New York City.

* * *

We hung up and all I could think about all night was "mountain girl" Cheryl, my sister, up in New York City all by herself. I knew she did the right thing getting away from Frederick. I did not think he could find her all the way up there, but leaving the baby was another thing all together, but I was not in her shoes. I knew she was scared to death of that man. He had killed once and he was not afraid to kill again.

The next night, I got another call from Cheryl. We talked till her dimes ran out for the pay phone. She begged me to come to New York, told me all about the big city, the subways, the tall buildings, everything. Washington was big, but Cheryl made New York out to be more exciting than Washington, D. C.

When I got off the phone, Lois asked me, "Do you want to go to New York to be with your sister? If you do, I will call Emily and Terry to see if they want to let you go all the way up there." I thought only a second and said, "She is so alone up there all by herself. Yes, I need to be up in New York with her."

Lois said, "Okay. That is settled. You can go. We must ask Terry and Emily first."

I said, "But who will watch the children for you?"

"Do not worry," she said. "School is almost out. I will be here with them. Also in a few weeks, we will be going back to North Carolina to the farm for the season. So, do not worry. If you want to go, then go."

She called Mama and Mama said that she was happy that I was going to go for Cheryl needed me to be with her. Two days later, I said good bye to all the children. Richard gave me some more money and put me on a train. I was off to the big city. You would never think a mountain moonshiner's daughter would be going to New York City. My, what a sight! I still dressed like a country girl, even with the clothing Lois had given me.

The train ride was good. Before too long, we were pulling into the Grand Central Train Station in the Big Apple. I got out of the train with all my cases. I had a big load. I could hardly walk. I wondered where Cheryl was with thousands of people going in every which a way. She had told me she would meet me when I got off the train. I did not know which way to walk. I start walking from the train with all kinds of people not paying me any attention. They walked like they were going to a fire or running from something. In all my life, I had never seen so many people.

I tied one of my belts around one of the cases and pulled it along. I had one small one under my arm and a larger one in my hand. I knew I looked a sight, dragging that large suitcase along and all, but no one paid me any attention. It was as if I was invisible.

I finally got to this real big room. People were still going ever which a way. I walked over to some benches and sat down. I

Mary Judith Messer

was sitting for about ten minutes when I heard Cheryl call my name. She was coming from across the big room.

"Judith! Judith!" I heard her calling. You talk about being glad to see someone, I am here to tell you, I was the one. I ran to her and we both hugged and hugged.

She had this real long dress on. She looked like she was still up on that mountain. She talked a mile a minute. She told me all about the big city. She said after she got the bus tickets up at Mama's mail box, she hid them from Frederick until the day she ran away to catch a Trailways Bus.

She got to New York and someone from the agency that sent the bus tickets was at the bus station to pick her up. Cheryl seemed to know where she was going. I sure didn't. We got out on the street and started walking. We walked down the street only a short time.

She told me she lived in a bad place and it only had one room. She stopped outside this building and started down some steps, around five steps. As soon as we were at the bottom of the steps, she had a key for a door and she opened the door to let us into the room. I will never forget how surprised I was.

New York Life & No Grits

Cheryl lived in a rat hole. We could not even see into the room, the one dim light bulb was so dirty and little. It had just one bed; not another thing in that room but Cheryl's clothing. Before we opened the door, we saw this rat run up the steps. I had always thought New York was all glamorous and pretty and new. I sure had something to learn about this big city.

Cheryl told me why she was not living with the people that the agency put her with. She said, "I was living with the first people, a family, with three kids. I was taking care of the children. I had been with them only two weeks when I saw all these real pretty clothing the lady was wearing."

She looked in the lady's closet while she was at work. She got herself a few things and hid them in a brown paper bag because she was in New York without any clothing at all. She only had the dress on her back, the one she wore in the North Carolina mountains. "I sure needed those clothes bad," she said, "or I would never have stolen them. It cost me my job and I was making twenty dollars a week." She said the lady missed her clothing and did a search in Cheryl's room. She found the clothing and fired Cheryl.

She said the agency put her with another family taking care of one child and cleaning the house. She said she left that place. She got fifty dollars from this man. She stole it when the man left his billfold lying on the table. She took that money and left the place. She was at that place only two months. She was making fifteen dollars a week.

She had taken the money to pay for the place and we stayed there only one night. Rats were too good to live in that dump.

We went looking for us a better place. We walked up one block after another. We finally saw a sign in a window that read, "Room to Rent." We went in. The old man at a desk talked to us. He said, "Just the room is thirty-five dollars a week. No bath, only rest room."

We went ahead and rented it for a week because it was getting real late. We were so tired. We had looked all day, walking up one street and down another one. We went back to the rat hole for our things. When we finally get everything moved in, we just fell into bed. We were so tired. We got woken up the next morning from all the sounds, subways, car horns blowing, and people talking! All that noise.

Cheryl and I went out. We looked for someplace to eat. I had not had a bite since I left Washington. We found a small restaurant only a block from the room. Cheryl had paid for the room for a week. I told her I would pay for our food for a week. We ordered eggs, biscuits, sausage gravy and grits.

The woman looked at us like we were crazy. She said, "No grits."

I said, "Where do you buy grits here?"

She laughed. "You must be from the south. We don't have grits here."

They did not even have them in the grocery stores. I guess they didn't even know what they were. I told Cheryl on the way up to Washington, Richard always stopped for breakfast at Howard Johnson's Restaurant. They always had grits. Cheryl said, "But, this is New York, not Virginia, where all of the Howard Johnson Restaurants are.

Even without grits, boy, that food was good! The milk was a little tasteless; I had drunk raw, natural cow's milk all my life which was wonderful, but no chance of getting that in New York! All the other food was so good, though. We ate till we popped and then we went back to our room where we just sat at the window and watched out at all the people, thousands of them, walking all over the streets. There was nothing else to do.

Moonshiner's Daughter

There was one radio in the room on a little table beside the bed. You had to put a nickel in it to get it to play. You dropped in your nickel and it came on and you turned the knob till you found the music you wanted to hear. We could never find country on the thing so we never wasted our nickels much. The radio played one hour for five cents. Then it shut off.

At night, we went back to the little restaurant where we got a cheeseburger and French fries. We walked around looking at all the tall buildings. We wondered what they were all for. We tried to learn the blocks, 34th Street, west, 24th Street, south. We needed to learn as much as we could. We knew we had to find jobs. Our money was getting low.

The next day, we walked and walked looking for somewhere to work. We walked in and out of restaurants looking for work, any work. We were willing to work at any jobs. We needed jobs bad. Finally we walked into this big restaurant together called the Horn and Hardart's. They told Cheryl she could work, but they told me I was too young and besides, I didn't have a Social Security Card. The agency that had sent Cheryl her bus ticket had helped her get her Social Security Card.

I was very sad. What would I do for money? I had spent all my money on food. All I had left was two big jars of dimes. The lady that hired Cheryl told me to go to the Social Security Office for my card, "But you are still under age for us to work you."

The next day, Cheryl had to be at the Horn and Hardart's at 7 o'clock. She was to help make the salads. Cheryl said, "We must look for a place to live that is a lot closer to the work."

We went about five blocks and saw a "For Rent" sign. We went in to see the landlady. She was very old and fat. She had all kind of boxes of food all over the room. She told us we could go up to look at the room.

It was up two flights of old wooden stairs that creaked when you walked up and down on them. The room was very small and not nice at all. Cheryl said, "Let's see how much she is renting it for."

"Okay," I said. "Let's go."

"Well, how do you like it?" the landlady asked.

Mary Judith Messer

"It's okay," Cheryl said, "but we will have to clean it up. How much is it?"

She said, "Fifteen dollars a week."

I told Cheryl, "Let's take it for it is costing us thirty-five a week for the other place." I thought we sure were getting more for our money. Then I asked, "But where do we use the bathroom and take baths?"

She said, "The rest room is down on the second floor down the hallway."

"Okay, okay," Cheryl said. "We will take it, won't we Judith?"

I said, "Okay," so we told the landlady. We said we would come back soon for we had to go get our money and our things from the other place.

* * *

We hurried back to the other rooming house and went to the landlord's office.

Cheryl said, "Sir, we need to get back our rent money. We only stayed two nights. We found us another place that is closer to my work. You owe us twenty-five dollars. We need it to pay the landlady at the other place."

He just stared at us. Then he said, "No refunds. We do not give refunds."

"But we need that money for our other rent," Cheryl told him.

"It is our money," I said. "You need to give it back now."

He said, "Where the hell do you get off, country hick, talking to me like that? Get the hell out of here before I call the cops!"

Cheryl and I started running for the door. She was already out in the hall when I turned around and shouted, "I bet you go to that hell you were talking about!"

He started towards me but I was already out the door. We got our things out of the room and took off. It was five long blocks to the other place and we had to lug all our things without any help. I

Moonshiner's Daughter

had to count out my dimes to pay the landlady for a week's rent. I was so glad that I had fifteen dollars in dimes and lots more. I had two jars full.

I asked Cheryl what a "hick" was and she said she didn't know.

Mary Judith Messer

Lost In New York &
My Social Security Card

We sat all our things in the new room and went to look for the rest room. My G…, what a mess! That bath tub was as yellow as it could be. The toilet itself was just filthy. I had been with Lois a good long time and she had taught me how to be good and clean. She made sure her bathrooms were always spotless. I do not think Cheryl was in as big a shock as I was at how dirty the bathroom was, but she was also in shock.

We needed to take us a bath bad and we sure could not take one in that nasty place. We got us some Ajax and Clorox and other cleansers from the landlady. We scrubbed with cleaner and steel wool till it made our hands raw. That bathtub and sink were old, but we got it as clean as we could. We both knew all about hard work and that was hard. We each took us a good bath we both deserved.

The bedroom was yet another thing. We never had time to clean it the day we moved in for it had taken all evening to clean the bathroom. In the room we only had time to make up the bed. That night we were eaten alive by bed bugs. Cheryl and I could not sleep at all. The next morning she was off to work. I went to see the landlady about the bugs.

She said, "I don't have any spray, but you can walk down a block to the A & P Grocery Store for some." She gave me two dollars and off I went.

As soon as I got out on the street, I saw all these men just standing around. They were speaking Spanish. I could not understand a word they said. I knew they were talking about me for they were watching me as they talked and laughed.

I started walking down the block. I could see the A & P and I crossed over to it. Many different kinds of men were standing in front of it and they were also speaking Spanish. They looked at me and talked and laughed. I wondered what was so funny. I did not think I looked funny.

I tried to get by them to go in the store. One stuck out his foot. I just stepped into the street and around his foot. Then they all laughed, like it was a big joke. As I came back up on the sidewalk, the same one did it again. He put his foot in front of me.

I said, "You better get out my way." I didn't think they knew what I said. I walked out in the street again. When I stepped back up on the sidewalk again, he let me go into the A & P. Inside, I bought two cans of bug killer and then went back out of the store.

By this time, the men had moved on down the street. I started down the block and saw them watching me and laughing. I crossed over to the other side of the street. They all crossed across also. I walked faster. They walked faster. I went back across the street. They walked back across the street. They did this till I was back at the door to the rooming house.

I sure was glad to get back to the room. I gave the change to the landlady and went upstairs. Right down below our room was a bar where men went in and out of all day and night. You could smell the beer upstairs in our room. I just hated any kind of alcohol and couldn't even stand the smell of it. I think it was because Daddy and Mama were such drunks.

Back in our room, I took off all the sheets and cover. I hauled them down to the bathroom and put them all in the bathtub. I poured some of the Clorox into the hot water, and some suds also. I left it all to soak.

I went to the room and sprayed all over the bed with the bug spray. Not one inch did I miss. I even wet the corners of the bed with the spray. I started coughing and had to raise the window even though the juke box playing down in the bar was really loud.

At four o'clock, Cheryl got back home. She liked the way I had cleaned up the room.

Mary Judith Messer

She helped me get the bed covers out of the bath tub. We rung them out the best we could and took them up to the room and hung them around the room to dry. We knew better than leave them in the bathroom to dry. Everybody living there used the same bathroom and   someone would have taken them.

We lay in that bed without any covers at all that night, but the bed bugs did not bite. We were just dead tired from not getting any sleep the night before and not even the loud music below could keep us awake.

Cheryl had brought me some food from Horn & Hardart's. I was very hungry and I ate it all. She got all the good food she wanted free.

The next morning, she left at 6:30 to walk to her job. I told her I was going to look for the Social Security Office. She didn't want me to leave the room after I told her about all those men who talked Spanish and how they followed me, but I had a mind of my own and I knew I needed a Social Security Card bad.

Cheryl said, "I have been begging my boss to hire you if you get a card." She had told Cheryl that she was afraid she would get into trouble with the law if she hired underage people.

Cheryl liked her job and she said making salads was fun. The best part, she got paid and free food. I wanted free food also.

I asked the landlady where the Social Security Office was.

She tried to tell me. "Go down to the subway. Take the subway to some street. Get off and go up steps into the street. Ask someone where it is. When you get out of the subway, it should be a block or two on that street."

I got dressed and went out to find the Social Security Office. My Lord, I sure didn't know New York was so big. Guess what? Yes, I got lost and bad lost. I went past my station and got off at the wrong station. I had to pay fifteen cents and get another token. I got on the wrong train again. It never stopped at my station. I had to go outside a station and walk a block and go into the subway again. Fifteen cents more for another train.

I must have asked a dozen people for directions; most were too much in a hurry to tell me which train to get back on. One black man finally told me the best way to go. I had left the rooming house at 7:30 that morning. When I finally got directions to the Social Security Office it was 3:45 in the afternoon and I still had to walk twenty-two blocks to get to there. I did get my card, but going back to the rooming house was another thing.

You guessed it! I got lost again. I got back to the rooming house at 11:30 that night. Cheryl was standing in the window, scared to death for what might have happened to me, when she finally saw me coming down the street in front of the house. I was so tired, I could not even climb the stairs. I crawled up them on my hands and knees. That was some trip. I made a promise to Cheryl that I would never go out on my own again like that (but I did).

At last, Cheryl had worked a whole week and she got paid. They were going to hold out a week on her, but she told them she needed the money. She told me that she would ask again if I could work too. She had a white dress she worked in and she looked good.

The next day, to kill time while Cheryl worked, I took fifty cents and went one block from the rooming house to see a movie playing at a second run theater. It was not hard to pick the movie I was going to see. It was Susan Haywood in *Come Back Little Sheba*. It was so sad. I cried all the way through it. Susan Haywood was so good. I loved the whole movie.

On Saturdays, we would sit on the bed looking out the window to the busy street below. We could hear everybody down on the street talking, mostly men, all speaking Spanish. We just looked and listened.

One guy came out of the bar below us. We saw him holding his arm behind his back. We could see his hand also and in it he had a knife. He walked up to this guy with a red cap and jabbed the knife in him three licks. We saw his blood everywhere. He first bent down to his knees, then fell face down on the sidewalk.

We didn't see what happened to all the other guys. They went off so fast. The guy that stabbed the one lying on the sidewalk ran down the block into the A & P. We saw him go out a side door at the A & P. Soon, police were all over the place. We never wanted

Mary Judith Messer

the police or anyone to know we saw what had happened. We were living in a real bad place. We were afraid we would be killed if we talked to the police in front of our rooming house.

A Job & A Party Invitation

To the left of our street was a small restaurant. On the weekends when Cheryl was off, we sometimes went there to eat. Everything was very greasy, the cheese burgers and everything were greasy, but the restaurant was handy so we ate there.

One evening after work Cheryl came in and said, "You can go in the morning to work with me. The boss lady said you can work on one condition: if you are asked your age, you must tell everyone you are eighteen years old. She said if anyone finds out you are under age, you will be fired and she will get into bad trouble."

I was almost jumping up and down, I was so happy. I needed money bad and I wanted to eat free. It was only four blocks to the Horn & Hardart's Restaurant.

Cheryl and I worked the same hours. I had to put baked beans and hot dogs and all kind of other dishes in these hot food machines. People on the other side of the machine would put change into them and pull out a nice warm dish of food. The food was very good and very reasonable priced. Thirty-five cents would buy the baked beans and hot dogs. Every time someone took out some food, I put more in. It was not a bad job.

Cheryl had learned how to make good salads and Jell-O. She sometimes dipped out food on people's plates when they told her what they wanted. We both were given white uniforms and I had to get white shoes like Cheryl's.

Each week when we got paid, we went to Times Square and 42nd Street. Down the whole block was one movie house after another all showing different movies.

We would stand on the sidewalk and look through the window as the Pizza man rolled his dough. He would also throw it into the air and catch it.

At another window, a man made fudge candy. He took this huge steel pot and poured out a long line of chocolate into a really big pan to be cut into small squares. He also made taffy candy. We had fun watching.

We walked up and down Times Square. It was just great for two mountain girls to see all the excitement. The lights were flashing off and on. When we got tired, we went to one of the movies.

I started getting real brave again and going to the movies at Times Square by myself. Cheryl did not want to go so I hopped on the subway and went alone. I was walking up the sidewalk on 42nd Street and was heading up the block to the movie houses when a man said, "Hello." He started talking about all kinds of things. "How old are you? I bet you are from Ireland, aren't you?"

I said, "No, from the south."

"You sure fooled me. You talk like you are Irish. Where are you headed?" he asked.

"I am going to see a movie."

"Why don't you come across the street? You know I make beautiful pure copper jewelry. Come on. I have a store and it is full of copper jewelry," he said.

I followed him across the street. He turned left then told me, "Here we are. Come on in."

I walked into the jewelry store. A man was working in the store. He was selling a young couple some necklaces and other items. He had all kinds of jewelry in showcases up one wall and down the other. It was all so beautiful. The man had told me his name was John.

I asked John, "How much is that necklace?"

He said, "That one cost twenty dollars." He took it out of the showcase and handed it to me. I put it around my neck, but I could not get it fastened. He said, "Here, let me fasten it for you."

He walked behind me and hooked the necklace. He showed me in the mirror, "Look how pretty you look with it. You are so beautiful."

I felt like sinking into the floor. Never in my whole life had anyone said I was pretty, let alone beautiful.

John opened his other showcases and got out all kinds of jewelry. He laid it on his showcase top and said, "You wait here. I will be back in a minute." The other man left the store to get something to eat. John was back in a few minutes. He had a bag that had all kinds of copper jewelry and also some brass jewelry inside. He picked up all the jewelry on top of the showcase and put it in the bag, too.

He said, "Here Judith. This is for the most beautiful girl I have ever seen."

I said, "Oh no. I do not have any money for it. You have put over one hundred dollars worth in the bag." I tried to take off the necklace.

He said, "Yes and it is all yours." He handed me the bag, but I wouldn't take it. He tried again to get me to take it. Then he reached for my purse on my side and dropped it in.

I just stood looking at him. He was around thirty five years old. *Why was he giving me all this jewelry? Maybe these New York people were just good hearted or something.* I just did not know. No one had come into the shop while the salesman had gone to eat. Not one person.

I felt pretty good about John and I guess he could tell.

He started smiling and said, "Judith, do you like parties? We, me and a bunch of good friends, mostly women, are having this great party Saturday night. Would you like to come?"

I said, "I do not know if I like them. I have only been to birthday parties of the children I used to live with."

He said, "Will you come tomorrow night, Saturday night? It won't be a birthday party, but you will just love this party."

I said, "It won't be a party like my mother used to call a party, with drinking moonshine and all will it?"

Mary Judith Messer

He looked at me, "Moonshine?" He said. "Do you mean illegal liquor?" He laughed. "No, no, no liquor at this party."

I was okay now with the idea of his kind of a party. I think we will have cake, ice cream all those good things we always had at the Queen children's parties; not a birthday party, but almost a birthday party.

I said, "But John, I don't know the way. I get so lost here in New York. I just know how to come to 42nd Street and Times Square by myself."

"Do not worry. You just come here at this store at 8 pm tomorrow night. Okay? I will take you to the party myself."

"Okay," I said, "I hope my sister, Cheryl, don't get mad at me for going out. She never even wanted me to go out by myself tonight, but I did anyway."

"Well," John said, "you are a big girl now. You do what you want to."

"I even have a job now. I am a big girl," I said.

He told me goodnight and I left. I walked across the street to all the movie houses. I looked in the ticket room and saw that the lady had closed her shade. The last shows had started. She was not selling anymore tickets, but I didn't get mad. I couldn't wait to get home and show Cheryl all my nice jewelry.

When I got to the room, it was past 11 pm. Cheryl was setting on the bed. Boy, was she mad at me. She never even looked at my jewelry. She said, "You will get killed up here. I told Mama I would look after you. Lois has always looked after you, now I am trying to keep you safe. Do you not understand, this is a bad place with lots of bad people?"

I tried to talk to her to tell her I got bored staying in this little room all the time. She was so mad I decided not to tell her about the party the next night. I would wait till I was ready to leave before I would tell her.

Fooled Again & Coney Island

Saturday night, Cheryl had already gone to bed and it was only seven pm. I told her I was going out. She sat straight up. "Where do you think you are going?" she said.

"I have been invited to a party. If you want to, you can come too!"

She jumped up. "You are not going anywhere!" she said. "Don't go out that door!"

She meant what she said, but I walked out anyway. I took the subway to 42nd and Times Square. I thought while I was on the train, *she could have come also. I told her she could. Why does she always have to stay in that old small room every night? I want to have fun.*

I got to the Jewelry Store and John came up to me right away.

"Hi," he said. "You look pretty in that blue dress."

"Thank you," I stammered, still not used to a compliment.

"Ten more minutes and my partner will watch the store and we will be off. My jewelry looks good on you. How did your sister like it?"

"She never looked at it."

"Let me give you a bracelet for her. You know we make all our jewelry ourselves."

He went behind the showcase and opened it.

I said, "No, I can give her a piece of mine."

It was too late because he laid a beautiful copper bracelet on the top. Then he handed it to me.

I thought *this one is prettier than mine.* It had a forty-five dollar tag on it. At that time, the fifties, that was big money.

John and I left the store. He flagged down a cab on the corner. He was talking to me small talk as we rode along in the cab. It was a good distance, we were going. I never knew where he was taking me, somewhere in Queens he called it. It took us longer than thirty minutes and finally we pulled up in front of some apartment buildings.

John got out. I started to open the door to the cab, but he had come around and opened the door for me.

I thought *he is a nice gentleman.* He took me into the apartment house. It was real nice, but no elevator. We walked up around four flights of steps. The building may have had an elevator, but I never saw one.

John came to a door on the fourth floor. He tapped with his fingers one time. The door opened. A man was standing inside. John and I walked in. Inside was a chair. John said, "Sit here. I will be back in a minute."

This man's name was Joe. I think *no music?* I asked Joe, "Where are the people?"

He said, "What people?"

I said, "This is where the party is, isn't it?"

"Oh, yes," Joe said. "The people have not got here yet."

I just sat down in the chair, and then Joe went into another room. I could see down the hall. The lights were all out. I stood up after a few minutes and wondered where John was. The older man, Joe, said, "He has gone to the kitchen to get us something to drink."

I walked down the hall and took a few steps into a dark room. I could see a bed and on the ceiling were bright shining stars, twinkling. Joe met me in the hall and said, "You want to have some fun?"

I said, "What kind of fun? Where is John? I came here to a party."

He said, "John had to go out for some more chips and Cokes."

"I never saw him leave," I said,

"Oh, he went out the side door."

"When are all the people coming to the party?" I asked.

Moonshiner's Daughter

"They'll be coming shortly," he said. "Now you and I can have some fun while we are waiting on them to get here." He took hold of my arm and pulled me into the dark room with the stars.

I tried to pull away, but he had hold of my arm good. "I do not want to have fun with you! Turn my arm loose!" I twisted my arm out of his and kicked his leg. He lost his grip and I ran for the door. He had fallen backwards a little and almost lost his balance. I got the latch open on the door someone had locked. Joe was right behind me, trying to get hold of my arms. I went out the door and ran down the hall. I got to the top of the steps when he kicked me with his foot in the back.

I fell down the first set of steps, but I got up fast as I could. I started down the second steps with him right behind me. He put his foot once again in my back. I went tumbling down two more sets of steps. It knocked the breath out of me and my arm felt like it was broken. I got to my feet and jumped the other steps. I hit the bottom steps and tripped and landed on my face. I lost the feeling in my arm and face. I stumbled through the door out to the sidewalk, barely hopping. It felt like my leg was broken. I hobbled on as fast as I could which was not fast for I hurt all over my body. I got a block away and finally looked back. I did not see him, but I thought *he may still be after me.* I was all out of breath, but I just kept going.

I didn't know the time and I didn't see many people out in this part of the city so I figured it must be pretty late. I walked block after block. I hurt so bad. I had no way of telling where I was or how far away a subway was. I walked over twenty blocks looking every minute behind me.

I finally found a subway, but I did not know which one to take back to Manhattan. I was so scared I was shaking. My hip and legs hurt so bad. A couple of people were waiting on the subway. I asked which train I should take back to Manhattan. They told me I needed to go back up and go over the street and take the other train because this one was not running to Manhattan. I had to pull on the banister to get back up the steps. They watched me and didn't ever ask a thing about me being injured. I knew I had blood on my face because my nose was still bleeding some, and when I put my hand on

Mary Judith Messer

my face, it felt like there was no skin on the right side and it burned like fire, but I was happy anyways for the help they gave.

On the train back to Manhattan, I started to cry. I was hurting so bad. I should have listened to Cheryl. I would not be hurt. *I almost got raped*, I thought to myself, and by a man old enough to be my father. I was still very afraid. I thought that Joe might follow me to the rooming house and kill me.

A few people were on the train. No one asked me what was wrong or why I was crying. They looked and then turned their heads. I thought *I could be lying on the floor dying and you would just look away*. I thought *I sure need to grow up fast in this city or I will be dead*. I watched everyone to make sure it wasn't Joe who had followed me.

I finally got back to our room. I was still crying. Cheryl never said anything. She had been sitting up waiting on me.

I told her everything that had happened to me. She ran to the window to see if anyone was watching us and pulled down the window shade. She was shaking all over. I was just so afraid Joe had followed me home. For a long time after that, I wouldn't go outside the building. I didn't even go to work. My lips were black and blue. Cheryl stayed out with me for two weeks, until we ran out of money. We did not know what we were going to do. Cheryl and I both got fired for staying out of work, of course.

* * *

Cheryl then got a job not too far from the Horn & Hardart's. It was in a candy making company called Schrafft's Candy Company. She was trained to make cookies and pack them in a box. They never hired me for they never needed another person. They said when they needed someone, they would tell Cheryl to bring me into work.

I went looking for me a job. This man stopped me on the sidewalk. I started to walk away and he said, "Miss, you want to make a lot of money?"

I looked at him and said, "I am now looking for a job."

He said, "I train women to be wrestlers."

I said, "I am not a woman."

Moonshiner's Daughter

He said, "How old are you anyways?"

I told him, "Seventeen."

He said, "That's okay. You can still be a wrestler."

I thought for half a second and said, "No, thank you" and walked off. I went down to Wall Street and went to an Employment Agency and gave them ten dollars I had gotten from Cheryl. They sent me to the Cardinal Card Company on Wall Street. It was easy to find and the lady receptionist was nice. She showed me what I was to do. I was so happy and asked her, "You mean, I am hired?".

She said, "Yes." She took my Social Security Number and all I had to fill out was a paper with my name and address and I was hired. My boss lady showed me how to line up cards and paste them into these big card albums. They mailed the card albums out to people all over the United States for them to see samples of the pretty cards so they could order what they wanted. I had a very easy job. When I told Cheryl that evening, she just thought it was great. I also told Cheryl about that man wanting me to be a wrestler.

Cheryl laughed her head off. "You could not stand the pain," she said. "They would kill you."

Cheryl and I thought we needed to become more beautiful. We found a beauty shop and we both got our hair cut and fixed. I thought we both looked pretty sharp. We did not go back to Times Square for a long time. We were afraid of that Joe and John. I knew after what had happened to me, I should have never took the jewelry from John. He thought that by me doing that, his friend or Daddy or whoever that Joe man was could have his way with me.

We jumped on the subway and took off to Coney Island. Someone at Cheryl's work told her about it. What a fun place! We rode all the rides. We ate hot dogs at Nathan's, best hot dogs in the whole wide world. It was just paradise for Cheryl and me.

We would walk up and down the boardwalk and look out over the ocean. When we got tired, we would sit down and eat some cotton candy. We just loved to watch as thousands of people walked down the boardwalk.

Mary Judith Messer

For two country girls, this was living just great. We wasted all our money every week for quite a while, only holding out money for our rent.

I salute you, New York! This was taken after we had been there for a year and was beside Central Park. Some of the "mountain girl" had rubbed off of me; and I had learned some hard lessons.

More Jobs &
Lost Again In New York

I was still at the card company, when without warning, I was fired. The boss lady said she found out I was underage. I cried all the way back to the room. Cheryl was surprised to see me in before her. I always came in half an hour after her for I had a longer way home from work.

The next day, she told me not to worry. She was going to try to get me on at the Schrafft's Candy Company. She was all happy when she got in that evening. She had good news. I could go to work the next day at the Candy Company.

She said, "No matter what, no one is to know your age. On the paper you fill out, put down you were born on this date and write it on a small piece of paper and put it in your pocket." It had taken the Card company months to find out I was underage.

I went to work at the candy company. The boss lady put me in this room with a girl whose name was Sherrie. She showed me how to put the candy in little cups and pack them in boxes with so many on the bottom and so many on top and the kinds to put in each row.

Sherrie was from Scotland. She was a real nice person. Her husband was a musician. He played in bands. I sure liked The Candy Company. Sherrie and I ate candy when we wanted it, but we never ate much. We smelled it all day long and just didn't want to eat it that much. I told Sherrie I should not eat much candy or I would get fat legs. She laughed her head off because my legs were so skinny, like sticks. Later on when I went back to North Carolina, Sherrie wrote to me. She began: *Hi, Fat Legs.*

Almost every day, Sherrie brought me a sandwich, mostly roast beef. She put mustard on it. I just love it that way to this day.

One day she came in and told me, her and her husband were moving to California. Her husband had gotten a job with Lawrence Welk and he would be on T.V.

I was so very sorry to see her go. I almost cried.

She hugged me good bye and I gave her my address so she could write me.

The last I saw her she said, "Now, fat legs, don't cry and don't eat too much candy." She sent me her new address in California. She sent me all kinds of pictures of her in California and of her children when she had them. She was a true friend, the best one I ever had.

Cheryl was the first to be laid off. I worked on for two more weeks, and then I got laid off too.

We both went back to the Employment Agency and gave them ten dollars for each of us to find us other jobs. They send us upstate, close to the Niagara Falls. A man picked us up and four more people. He was taking us to this big boarding house to clean it up. He said he would pay us fifteen dollars a week and our room and board. The trip was long.

We finally got to his rooming house. It was very big and very dirty. No one had lived in it for over three years. It had three floors. He put two people on the 3rd floor and two people on the 2nd floor.

Cheryl and I worked on the first floor. We cleaned all day long, only stopping at lunchtime long enough to eat a sandwich. At night, it was sometimes hot and of course there was no air conditioning. It took us three and one half weeks to clean that place. The boss man saw we worked hard, and he never pushed us. He was okay. He drove us back to the city and gave us all a five dollar tip. Our land lady had held our room for us but we had to pay for the three and a half weeks rent while we were gone.

* * *

Moonshiner's Daughter

Back in our room, Cheryl said we would go to Coney Island to have some fun before we went back to the Employment Agency and we did. Two days later, we were back again at the Employment Agency, paid our money again (ten dollars each was a lot of money then). This time, we had to take all our things with us for we were to live in the Woodstock Hotel in Asbury Park, New Jersey. The Employment Agency gave us two tickets for the bus. We got all our things out of our room and said good bye to the landlady.

We got on the subway to get to the bus station. We were just plain loaded down. Cheryl now had a big suitcase and a pasteboard box. I had a box with all my records. We came to our stop and Cheryl stepped through the door onto the platform. The subway doors closed before I could get all my things up and out the door. The train took off and the last I saw of Cheryl was her screaming for me at that station. I didn't even know which station that was. She had the tickets and all the money. I did not even have another subway token.

At the next station, I got off and dragged my things up the long steps and out of the station to the street. I sat down at the top of the steps. People were running all over the place. I thought *Cheryl will come back for me if I sit and wait long enough.* I waited for over an hour, no Cheryl.

I walked down the street, dragging everything along. I came to a U. S. Post Office. I sat down on the steps and looked over everyone going by, hoping to see Cheryl. I was worried sick. It never occurred to me to ask anyone where the bus station was. I just never thought of it.

I was so worried and it was getting very late and dark. I walked up one block and down another. I was so tired and started crying. A man stopped in front of me. By now I was real afraid of most men. The man was trying to get me to stop crying. He couldn't understand what I was saying. I told him my sister was lost somewhere in New York. We were going to New Jersey and my sister had all the money and the bus tickets.

He said, "Okay. You need to get off this street. You are too young to be out here late at night. Around three blocks down the

Mary Judith Messer

street is the YWCA. Come on, I will help you carry your things. The people at the YWCA will let you stay there for free till you find your sister. Now stop crying and come on."

He had my suitcase and started going down the block with it. I followed him to the YWCA and he took me to a woman at a desk. "I found this young lady on the street crying. Can you take care of her?" he asked.

The nice looking lady came out from her desk. "Why, sure, I will help her. Thank you so much for bringing her in."

With that he told me, "Good luck finding your sister," and he was gone. What a kind man. There were good people in the city after all.

The lady asked me a hundred questions. She said, "You must be hungry." She had a man bring me some hot soup and a sandwich. I was very hungry, but I wondered how hungry Cheryl was.

The lady said, "That's okay. You can take it with you to your room. You may feel like eating it later."

"Okay." I shook my head, "Yes."

She rang a small bell and a man came in. He wore a red and blue outfit. She said to him, "Will you please take Judith up to the 3rd floor to room 318 and take her tray of food also?"

Then to me "Judith, if you want, you may eat breakfast down here in the morning."

The man took me to the room, and he gave me a key. Alone in my room, I cried almost all night. And I worried, *Where is Cheryl sleeping?* I just laid in the bed and cried, but finally fell asleep in the early morning.

As soon as it was daylight, I took the elevator down to the first floor, walked through the lobby and out the door. I left all my things in the room. I started walking, looking all over for Cheryl. I walked and walked. Finally, I got so tired, I found some steps and I sat on them for a long time. I got up and walked back the way I had come till I saw the YWCA. It was late. I had walked the streets all day long looking for her. I went back up to my room and cried myself to sleep, I was so tired.

I was so sound asleep that I never heard the lady knocking on my door. The next morning, I went to the lady. She said, "You know you sure were sleeping. I even peeped into your room and you never woke up. We are trying to find your sister. We have the law looking all over for her. Have you had anything to eat?"

I told her I could not eat, thinking my sister was hungry and lost. She marched me straight to the little kitchenette and sat me at a small table. She had some eggs, toast and a whole breakfast for me. She left me with the food to go and take care of her office.

I took one bite of the eggs and started crying again. I left the food and went out to the street. This time I walked a lot further. I got tired again so I sat down on some steps and looked across the street. The bus station was just on the other side. I got up and crossed the street.

I walked inside and it was so big, so many people walking everywhere. I saw just hundreds of all kinds of people and most of them pulling or carrying suitcases. I walked over to a bench and sat down.

All at once, I heard over the intercom: "Is Judith Long in the bus station? Please come to the information desk." Then I heard it again. I jumped up from the bench and asked a woman, "Where is the information desk?"

She said, "Down that way on the right."

I almost ran down to the desk. A lady and a man were at the desk and the lady said, "May I help you?"

I said, "Yes! Yes! I heard you calling my name on the loud speakers. What do you want with me? Have you found my sister? Is she here? Where is she?"

"Slow down. What is your name?" she asked.

I said, "Judith Long."

She came from behind her desk and asked the man she left there, "George, will you page Miss Long please?"

Then she told me the best news. "Yes, Judith. We have your sister. She has been in here looking and waiting for you for three days and nights."

Mary Judith Messer

The man George called over the loud speakers, "Will Miss Long come to the information desk, please. Miss Cheryl Long."

I waited for five minutes and then I took off looking for her. I walked through the long building. I saw the ladies room and went in. Cheryl was standing at the sink, washing her hands. I ran into her arms, both of us sobbing. Tears were running down our faces.

She said, "Judith, I have been here for three days and nights in this bus station. Every night I lay down and slept on these benches, hoping you would come in. I have been so worried. Every hour they have called your name over the speakers. At night I slept on the bench and a security guard watched over me. They have been good to me here."

I told her about the YWCA and we went and picked up all my things. I told the lady at the YWCA how thankful I was to her. Cheryl also told her how thankful she was. I found out later that all the law officers had been on the lookout for the lost girl. "ME."

A New Boardwalk & Greek Men

Cheryl and I finally got on the bus for Asbury Park, New Jersey and we rolled into the bus station in Asbury after a short while. We saw a beautiful, big beach and a boardwalk.

We started walking, lugging our cases and a pasteboard box with my records. Every few steps, we sat our things down and rested. We must have just looked a sight to other people with all our things lugging them along. It took us a good hour to find the place and we had to ask six people.

We saw this huge hotel, just beautiful with all white wood. It had over a thousand windows. This place we were told was built in the 1800's. What a sight.

Cheryl and I walked into the lobby and lots of Guests were sitting in there reading papers and smoking pipes or watching T.V.

This is living, I thought. We walked over to the desk and a woman looked down at us. "What do you need?" she asked. We sat our luggage down; I was still holding my box of records. We told her we came from the Employment Agency for the maid jobs. She said she would tell the lady, Mrs. Hyatt. She was the one who hired and fired. "Please take your things and wait in the hallway on the left."

We did as we were told and stood in the hallway for over an hour. This lady finally came to us and said, "I am Mrs. Hyatt. Why are you three days late? I do not think I can use you now. We needed maids three days ago, not now."

Cheryl said, "Oh, please Mrs. Hyatt!" and told her why we were late. "We are out of money and had to pay ten dollars each to the Employment Agency. We don't have a return bus ticket. Please give us our jobs," she begged. "I do not know what we will do. We have no money for our rent or anything."

Mrs. Hyatt said, "You are well aware that your sister here cannot work? She is underage." I wondered how she knew my age?

I said, "What will we do, Cheryl?"

Cheryl said, "Why did the Employment Agency take her money? They sent her on this job also, for I would not have come if she was unable to work. Mrs. Hyatt, please let us work."

"Okay, okay." Mrs. Hyatt said. "I will hire you but not your sister. I do not need trouble from the State. She may stay in the room with you and get one meal a day free. We will take out of your check for your room and board."

Mrs. Hyatt had a man take us up to the room, all the way to the top floor. What a room. It was so small and so hot, only one bed in the room.

I told Cheryl "I sure hope all the rooms in the hotel are better than this one."

She said, "This floor is where the maids and bus boys stay. The other guest rooms are better, I am sure."

Cheryl was put right to work. I was left in that very hot room. Water just poured off of me. I opened the door to get a little air, but the hallway was just as hot. The one small window never opened. I laid on the bed and looked at my picture albums I had with me, all kinds of pictures of all the Queen children in Virginia and on the farm in North Carolina. The albums were my treasures. I still have them today.

I didn't know what to do with myself. There was nothing to do, no T.V. We could not even play our few records. It was so boring in that place.

Cheryl had a fifteen minute break. She came up to check on me. I was laying on the bed looking at the walls.

She said, "The maid work is okay."

I told her, "I am not going to just stay in this sweat box of a room. Tomorrow I am going outside to see what I can see."

That evening, every room on that floor had the doors open all night long. It was so hot, you could not sleep.

Cheryl said, "All the other rooms on the lower floors have air conditioning and the rooms all are so nice." The guests gave Cheryl tips. She had another maid help train her till she could do it all by herself.

I wanted to work so bad. I needed money. I chose to take my one free meal a day at suppertime. Some days, I was very hungry waiting for suppertime to come. Cheryl and I never had any money. The fourth day, some people left the hotel and left Cheryl a twenty dollar tip. Now that was good money for the fifties.

Cheryl thought she was going to get rich at this place. She gave me five dollars so I might go out and get a hot dog or French fries. I went outside every day. I walked down to the ocean. I loved the ocean. I walked in the sand. It was great, but it would have been so much better if I could have worked in the days and come to the beach at night with Cheryl. I would have been so much happier.

One day I walked up the boardwalk and into all the shops. Asbury Park had all kinds of gift shops. You could buy lots of things with Asbury Park on them. I saw this photo album. I still had the five dollars Cheryl had given me. I was keeping it for hard times. That day must have been a hard time day for I bought one of the photo albums.

The next day, I stayed in the room and put the rest of my photos in the album. Every night Cheryl and I went down to the beach. We sat with our feet in the water. It got cool at night on the beach. We loved to hear the water splash. We walked up and down in the sand. We saw lovers under the boardwalk. We didn't even think about boys. We were just happy to be together.

Cheryl worked at the hotel every day except Saturday and Sunday. We stayed on the beach all day long those days. One day I saw this door open at the end of our hallway. I walked down to the end to see what was out there. It was the fire escape and in case of a fire, you could climb down. I walked on out on the fire escape. Three bus boys were sitting out on it. They jumped when they saw me. They were all smoking.

They said, "Who are you? We thought you were old Mrs. Hyatt."

Mary Judith Messer

I talked to them some and saw it was a little cooler out there than in the room. I sat down with them, but I didn't smoke. I hated high places and tried not to look down.

They said, "We'll get fired if old Mrs. Hyatt finds us out here."

One told me to get up and close the door so no one would see them. I went out a lot on the fire escape, sometimes at night with Cheryl, when we were not on the beach. Every time we were out there, those boys were out smoking.

Cheryl worked at this grand old hotel for four months then she got laid off when the season ended, so back to the city we went. We got our room back. Cheryl and I went back to work at another Horn & Hardart's Automatic Restaurant. They never found out I was under age.

One day one of the boys that carried dirty dishes to the dumb waiter started to talk to me. His name was Alex. He was Greek. He sure was good looking. He had coal black hair and real dark eyes. He was a little short, but I still thought he was so cute.

Alex asked me out one night. I was so happy. Cheryl was not worried about me going with Alex for she had seen and talked to him a lot of times at the restaurant.

Alex got us a cab. It was Saturday night. We went to see a movie. He told me he had come from Greece with his dad when he was very small. He lived with his Daddy. His mother was dead. He spoke real good English. We had a good time. At the movies, he never even tried to kiss me, he just held my hand all the time at the movie and in the car. I thought *he must like me.*

At work, we talked some, but not too much. I guess Alex thought we might get fired. Three weeks later he asked me out again. This time he never said where he was taking me. Once again, he got us a cab. In the cab he said, "Have you eaten supper?"

"No, I haven't," I said.

"Well," he said, "my dad has cooked a big meal and I bet you have never eaten Greek food before. I am taking you to try out some. Okay?"

I said, "Great."

Moonshiner's Daughter

The taxi pulled to the front of this apartment house. It was not too many blocks from where we worked. We went up to the fourth floor in an elevator. We walked in and I first noticed how dark the living room to the kitchen was as we walked through. I could barely make out a bed in the left side of the living room.

Alex said his dad had to go out, but our food was still hot on the warmer. He had the lights on, but the rooms were dusty and dark.

He sat this small table with dishes and put all the food on the table. It was five dishes of different Greek food. He told me the names of each, which I forgot as soon as he told me. Anyway, it all looked good and I was hungry. I tried a little of all five dishes. It was all very good, but I would eat anything back then.

We talked for around half an hour after we put the dishes in the sink and the food was put away. We talked about my home town and the Queens who I lived with and all about Greece. He had only been to Greece one time since coming to America.

He started kissing me and putting his arms around me. He told me that was his bed over in the corner. He said his dad slept in the other room. By then, he was putting his hands all over me. He said, "Let's sit on the bed," and we went over and sat on the bed.

He said, "You know how we Greeks have sex?" I was getting embarrassed and never said a word.

He said, "We have sex behind."

I said, "Behind what? What are you talking about?"

He went on to tell me this and that. I was shocked, to say the least.

"No, no! I could never do that, Alex. Could you take me home?"

He said, "Okay, fine." He never tried to take advantage of me or anything. I guess it was because we both worked together. That was the end to Mr. Alex. I saw him at work, but we never spoke again. I thought *Greek men are crazy.*

Mary Judith Messer

Meeting Our Hero &
Cheryl Gets Bobbie Back

Cheryl and I met this man, Bill Donovan, at the restaurant. I was picking up the dishes on his table one day when he started to talk to me. Now Bill was this tall, slender man with a top hat, suit and a bow tie. I never one time saw him without his hat and bow tie. I thought he must put dye on his handlebar mustache. He was around forty-five when we met him. He talked to me every day when he came in to get his food.

One day he was waiting for Cheryl and me to get off of work. Cheryl was ashamed for him to know where we lived in that slum of a room.

Bill seemed to like Cheryl a lot. He told us, 'Surely you do not live in that part of the city. You girls do not need to be down there. I must get you out fast. How did you get in that part of the city anyway? All the Puerto Ricans live there."

The next day after work, he moved us out of Manhattan to the Bronx. He put us in this real nice neighborhood. The apartment was nice. We had an Italian landlady named Isabella. He paid the rent for us for six months at twenty dollars a week.

Cheryl and I had not gone out with Bill, not even one time at this time. He was just a great human being to us country girls in need and he was rich. He was a worker for the Merrill Lynch company. He made long trips all over the world as a sugar broker. He never talked about his family over in Ireland. He had been in the US since a very young boy. Bill was a true friend. We were back working at

Bill Donovan helped us find a pretty apartment and we finally started feeling at home. We even had a TV and a parakeet too!

another Horn & Hardart's Restaurant. They had them all over the city in the fifties. When we got in our own apartment, we had a little kitchen and a living room with Chinese wall paper and a nice overstuffed, purple, velvet couch. We had to use the same rest room as the other renters on the same floor, but it was so clean you could

Mary Judith Messer

see yourself in the sink and the tub was new looking. Cheryl and I even liked our little bedroom and it started to feel like a real home. We finally had a nice place in a very nice neighborhood. What more could we ask for? We worked every day except Saturday and Sunday. I saved every penny I could.

We still went to Coney Island for fun on the weekends. Bill just took Cheryl out three times. Cheryl was the kind of person that never liked the good night life. Bill took her to the best restaurants in the city and also to Radio City Music Hall. She just never liked the fancy places and never went out with Bill again. So when he was back in town from one of his out of town trips, he asked me, "Would you like to go out?"

Not one time did he take me just to the movies. He took me to eat at Jack Dempsey's Restaurant and lots of Broadway plays and Radio City Music Hall. Every time Bill came to the door to pick me up, he had a dozen red roses in his arms and, most of the time, a big box of candy also.

Bill never made a pass at me ever. One time, when he took me home in a cab, at my door he asked me, "If you don't care, will you let me give you a little kiss on the cheek?" I let him. He just barely touched his lips to my cheek and said, "Good night, Bunny." He called me Bunny all the time. They never made, in the whole wide world, a better man than Bill Donovan. He was my best friend in the whole wide world

Also, going out with Bill, I got to meet lots of movie stars, even Susan Haywood, and some gangsters, too, I thought. I sure was living it good.

At the Horn & Hardart's our boss's name was, yes…another Alex, and he was Greek also. He was around forty-five to fifty years old. He was a nice man. Alex was the head of the Greek Parade. Every year the Greek people in the city had a Greek parade. Alex took Cheryl and me home with him to meet his wife and family. He had us over to his house a lot. His wife cooked real good Greek food. They invited us over for the wedding of his niece. A Greek

Moonshiner's Daughter

wedding sure was nice. They had dancing and lots of good food. We really liked Alex and his whole family.

Alex introduced me to his nephew who was just in the U. S.

for a few months. He never spoke a word in English. He took me to see an American film. I knew he could not understand a word in the movie. He was a good Greek guy, but I only went with him one time. We could not communicate with each other. That was too bad for I would have liked to be in Alex's family.

Alex had Cheryl and me be part of the Greek parade. Cheryl's dress was made like the Greek flag. I was dressed like a Greek girl. I had on a velvet dress and vest with a little cap on my head with a gold sash. We marched down long streets and were very proud to be in the Greek parade. We went to Alex's house for a great meal afterwards. When Alex went to Greece, he mailed us a load of photos he had made in Greece. One was him on a donkey with his suit and tie. One was of a big Greek ship. There were all kinds of them. Alex was sure a great man and we liked him a lot. We had to borrow two hundred and fifty dollars from him because we had wasted the rent and subway money and could not get to work. We only asked him one time and he gave it to us right away. I was so

Mary Judith Messer

sorry we never paid back the money. We should have given it to him anyway when he came back to the United States.

I started saving up my money and stopped wasting it at Coney Island because I had one thing on my mind. I bought Cheryl a return bus ticket to North Carolina. I sent her to Waynesville to get that baby. She was very afraid of Frederick, but she went anyway.

Our plan was for her to go to Mama's house and get Mama and Daddy to go up on the mountain and get Frederick to let them bring Bobbie Lee to their house to spend the night with them. Cheryl was to stay hid and not let Frederick see her.

She got to Mama and Daddy's. They said they would do it. Frederick liked Mama and Daddy a lot. Daddy kept making moonshine with him even after Cheryl had run away.

Mama, Daddy and Cheryl drove up to the mountain. Cheryl hid in the floorboard of the car. They drove almost as far as the old shack then Daddy stopped in a deep curve so Frederick could not see the car. Daddy knew that Frederick had killed a man once and he would do it again if he had to.

Cheryl walked around the curve just enough to see the old shack. She could see the little boy playing out in the dirt. She got real scared and Daddy had to drive her back to their house.

Then, Mama and Daddy drove back up to the Holler Creek Mountain. Frederick let Bobbie come home with them, but Frederick also came.

Cheryl was hiding in the woods. When they got back, Cheryl was scared to death that Frederick would know she was there.

All this time I was in New York worried sick. I had made Cheryl promise she would call me as soon as she got the boy. He was now five years old and would not know who Cheryl was.

Daddy took Frederick to the store so Cheryl could see the boy and make the call to me. Cheryl was afraid to let the boy see her for he might tell Frederick there was a woman at his Grandma's. So she stayed hid. Mama put the phone out the window so she could call me. She called me in New York. I had stayed out of work to wait for her call.

When I finally got her call at 4:30, Cheryl was so scared she said she was not going to get the boy. I just blessed her out. I said, "I saved up that money all this time to get that baby. You do not come back up to New York without him and I mean it."

She was crying and I told her, "That boy needs his mother. Stop that crying and get him on the bus. What time is the Trailways running?"

She said, "At seven pm."

I said, "You and the baby better be on it!"

She said, "I have to hang up and get hid again. Daddy and Frederick will be back soon."

When they got back, Mama begged Frederick to let Bobbie stay all night with her for he had to go back to Holler Creek to look after his moonshine still.

He said, "Okay, he can stay but bring him home tomorrow."

Bobbie liked Mama and Daddy so Frederick let him stay.

As soon as Frederick left, Cheryl came out of hiding. She tried to hug and kiss Bobbie, but the boy wanted nothing to do with her. He cried and screamed his head off. She tried and tried to make friends with the boy. He had been up on that mountain so long, he was like a wild thing.

Daddy took Cheryl and Bobbie to the bus station and I got another call from her once again. She was too scared to get on the bus with the boy. She said they had to stop over in Asheville, North Carolina at the bus station. She was afraid Fredrick would follow her to Asheville and get her while she waited for the other bus. Now she was crying very bad. She wanted to let Daddy take the boy back home.

I told her again, "That is your son. Don't get on that bus without him."

She said, "Okay, okay."

She finally caught the bus but the boy wouldn't have a thing to do with her. He wouldn't talk to her or anything. She said he just said, "I want to go back up on the mountain."

Mary Judith Messer

When their bus rolled into the bus terminal, I was waiting because I had been watching every bus as it arrived. I could not wait to get to see my little nephew. I was so surprised when I did see the little fellow. He was so dirty. His clothing was too big and his hair was long and nasty. I ran and picked him up. I said, "I am your Aunt Judith."

He hugged my neck and said, "Aunt Judith, make that woman take me back to the mountains."

Cheryl said he had slept most the way, but he would not talk to her.

The first thing I did was buy him some new clothing. We gave him a good bath. He had never been in a tub of water before. He had never had cake or candy and ice cream. He was just a little mountain boy. Every day he wanted to stay next to me. He wanted nothing to do with his mother at all. He would ask me for water or whatever he wanted.

Cheryl got jealous of me because he liked me. She told me not to give him water or anything else. She wanted him to have to ask her for the things he needed. I was so sorry for him, I could have cried. He would do without before he would ask her for anything. It took weeks before he would call her Mama. He was so pitiful.

She would say, "You call me Mama. I am your Mama. If you want anything, you say, 'Mama, can I have some water?' or whatever you want."

Cheryl got the landlady, Isabella, to look after him for twenty dollars a week while we worked. In the evenings, we took him to the local playground. The first time he saw the black children at the playground, he just put his little hands over his mouth and eyes, he was so surprised. He had never seen black people before. I took all kinds of photos of him at the playground, some with the little black girls and he soon got used to them and they played in the sandbox together. We took him to the Bronx Zoo every Sunday. We liked it as much as he did. We loved the hotdogs and chips at the Zoo also.

On Saturdays, we went to Coney Island. Finally Bobbie Lee started to enjoy himself and he started calling Cheryl Mama. She was so happy, but it took Bobbie years before he would eat cake or candy.

Moonshiner's Daughter

Our little "cowboy" playing with some new friends in the neighborhood at the apartment playground.

My nephew and me all dressed up near our apartment. Once he got used to living with us he really enjoyed it.

My "glamour" shots in NYC as a teenager. Don't I look grown-up? The final shot is with my nephew now happy to join us in the city. Many of these pictures were taken before I went "out on the town" with my friend Bill Donovan.

Moonshiner's Daughter

Visitors From Home &
Expensive Pictures

The rent was twenty dollars a week and for Bobbie's keep with Isabella was twenty dollars. That was forty dollars a week. In the fifties, that was very big money to us girls. Mostly we paid on time.

That Isabella really hated me. She liked Cheryl a lot. I could never understand why she hated me so. She spoke good English but Italian sometimes, too. Then when she spoke English, she would take her fingers to her lips and say, "Cheryl is an angel. You are the devil." She never liked my rowdy ways. When I wanted to go out, I went out.

Cheryl never wanted me to leave the apartment at night, but I had a date with this boy. She never knew him much. He had only come up to the apartment one time. He just came in and sat on the couch until I got ready. For some reason, Cheryl never liked him, but I went out with him anyway.

Cheryl and I got into a big fight about him. We had fights before but we never hit each other with our hands or anything. This time it was different. I picked up a spoon off the table and threw it at her. I hit her right in her front tooth and chipped it. I was sorry I did that. I later cried about it.

Cheryl was now trying to look better. She had put this blond dye on her hair to lighten it but it turned her hair a sick-looking red blond. I never told her, but it just looked real bad.

She was getting up in the world. She had met this man named Herman. Herman lived at the Country Club upstate where he even had a tennis court. It would have been nice for her to marry a very rich man like Herman. He was a tall slender man around forty. He bought her all kinds of real expensive things. She only went out with him about five times. Then she said she didn't like him. She never saw him again.

I still went with Bill Donovan when he was in town. He bought me this beautiful mink coat, a furry white sweater, a shawl, just lots of real nice things. It was easy to think I owed him something for all the gifts, but Bill was never like that. I was so thankful that he was a real gentleman. Those kinds of people are real hard to find. He would say, "Bunny, why don't you come to Merrill Lynch to my office and be my secretary?"

I said, "But Bill, you know I can't type."

He would only say, "You don't have to type. Just come sit behind the desk and look pretty."

I never knew if he was just joking or not. I never took him up on the offer. I wanted so bad to go to Saudi Arabia. All the time I talked about going and working for the American Arabian Oil Company.

When I told Bill, he said, "Those old sheiks will steal my Bunny away, take you out in the desert to live in an old tent. I would never see you again." I just laughed.

In the next apartment down from us lived a man, woman and young son. They had worked in Arabia. They told us all about Arabia and the real great money you could make there, but you had to sign up for three to five years to go over or if you came back to the states, you had to pay your own air tickets. But with that kind of money you could well afford the air fare.

When I was out with Bill, we went into all the big stores, Macy's, Gimbals, all over the city. It was fun to see so many great things, but every time I would take interest in anything Bill would tell the sales lady, "Wrap it up". I got so I would not pay much attention to things for he would buy it every time and that would make me feel guilty. I would tell him I didn't want him to spend so much money

Moonshiner's Daughter

on me. He would just laugh and say, "Bunny, you know it's just cabbage. Don't worry!"

* * *

Sometimes on the weekends, Cheryl and I would go to the Radio City Music Hall by ourselves. We just loved to see the whole orchestra rise up from under the stage floor. And those Rockette dancers were just great. They threw up their legs all at one time, never missed a step. When Bill was out of town, we also liked to go to lots of plays on Broadway. We both had now learned how to maneuver in that big, great city. We started enjoying life after Bill got us out of the slums to the Bronx. We also went to lots of nice restaurants.

Mary Judith Messer

Cheryl had another hot date. She met this man from Upstate New York who was in the city to settle some wills with his lawyer. His wife had passed away and he was in the city on business. His name was Wayne.

Wayne was what you might call a great white hunter. He went to Canada every year to hunt big game. He had his den full of his trophies. He had a very big estate and was quite wealthy. He also had three grown children.

Cheryl and Wayne hit it off good. He took her to all kinds of nice places upstate. He always came to pick her up in a limousine. It was quite impressive to see that big long black car rolling into our neighborhood. Everyone would look.

Sometimes I got to go with them to Wayne's estate. Bobbie loved to ride in that long thing. Wayne gave all of his wife's things to Cheryl. She had a limousine full of real expensive clothing that had never been put on. She went with Wayne for two years. He wanted her to marry him, but that was not to be. His children were against it from the start. They all said she was too young for him. He was very heartbroken, but he brought her home one last time in the limousine. So, goodbye, Wayne.

* * *

I hadn't had much time to call Lois back in Virginia. I never knew if she was still there or in North Carolina and I knew she was always busy. We had a surprise call one day from Sam Junior., Richard's brother. He called us and told us he was in New York and Lois had asked him to check up on "us girls". She had been worried because she hadn't heard from us in a while. He was on his way to Panama with his wife Mary and their children Rachel and Joe Sam to teach school there.

We met Sam Junior and his family at a fancy restaurant in the city where they treated us to dinner. We were so happy and surprised to see someone from home that we knew, because we were so home sick. He and Mary asked us all kinds of questions because he said, "We are on a mission to check on you girls by order of Lois!" We answered all the questions, where we worked, how much money we made, where we lived and so on. The meal was great.

Sam Junior told us that his kids would like to go on the underground train, the subway, and would we take them so they could experience it. When we got to the underground subway station, and a subway came flying by, Joe, who was around three or four, was thrilled and couldn't wait to go. Rachel, who was a little older, got kind of scared by the speed and noise and said she didn't want to. Her Mama said that was okay, for us to go ahead and take Joe and Sam Junior. We did and they had a really fun time. Mary and Rachel waited for us to come back. Sam Junior gave us some spending money before he left and we were so grateful.

* * *

After the visit by Sam Junior and his family that we enjoyed so much, we got the idea to save up money and send Mama and Joanie a bus ticket to come to New York. It had been two Christmases since we had been able to go down to North Carolina to take gifts home and see them. We had mailed our Christmas gifts when we couldn't go down there.

We met Mama and Joanie at the bus station. We were so glad to see them. The first thing we did was take them to buy a dress for Mama and some pedal pushers and tops for Joanie.

Mama was glad to see Bobbie. She said, "He's so big now!"

Bobbie and Joanie played all over the place. We took them to the park and to the Bronx Zoo. Joanie was a real tomboy. She climbed up on this huge statue in Central Park and kissed the lips of the statue. Everyone was standing around looking at her and taking photos. She walked in the water at the fountain. People were taking her picture every minute. The little boy Maurice that lived next door to us was with us. Joanie and Maurice climbed up on top of the rock cliffs. The animals in the zoo were not wild, but Joanie sure was.

When we got back to the apartment, we all went up on the ten story roof top to get a good look at the city. Joanie took a leap and jumped across the top to the next building. Mama was just

Mary Judith Messer

screaming at her not to jump back. If she had missed the top of the other building, she would have fallen ten stories down into the alley. We got her down and fast. No, she was not retarded. She was just a crazy kid from the mountains.

We took Mama and Joanie to Coney Island. We knew they would love it. Joanie rode all the rides. Mama never got on a one. We ate cotton candy, hot dogs and everything. Then we let Mama hold onto Bobbie Lee and we got on the big Ferris wheel. When we were on the very top and the Ferris wheel stopped, we heard Mama crying out, "Get my girls down!" I had never liked high places. I knew better than to go on that thing or any fast ride so I don't know why I did.

She screamed for them to stop that wheel and let her girls off. The poor man that was running the wheel almost got beat up for Mama was swinging her pocket book at him. When he got us off, she was holding her heart and all, but it was a good thing she got him to stop it when she did.

The second I got off, I ran to the nearest trash can. I still got sick like I did when I was young when I was riding in a car around all those old steep curves in the mountains and I still hated high places.

Mama had run out of her snuff. We looked all over New York for the stuff. Most places never knew what snuff was. We finally found some but it was not her sweet kind. It was another brand, all together different from her sweet snuff she always dipped. That other brand was stale and it made her sick, but she went crazy without snuff so she tried to use it anyway.

At night we let her and Joanie sleep in our own bed, but she got mad because Cheryl, Bobbie and I had to sleep on the couch and floor. We tried to tell her to stay and sleep in the bed, but she wouldn't listen and she got on the floor also. What a Mama!

The next day we took them back to the zoo. We ate hot dogs till we burst. We just had a great time. Then came the day for them to catch the bus back to North Carolina. We had taken a week off from work to give them a good time. I think we surely did just that, but now, back to our peace and quiet.

Moonshiner's Daughter

It was so great to once again get to work. We were out of money and the rent needed to be paid. We got Bill to let us have some. He was only too glad to help us out. We were so happy he was in town when we needed him most. For Bill, he made us a gift of the money and he told us it was a gift when he gave it to us. Bill met my Mother and she said she liked him and made him promise to look after her girls. He told her he surely would do that.

Cheryl met another man. I do not recall his name, but he worked for the railways. He had this blue uniform on and was very good looking. He was tall, real dark, dark black hair, but you could not see it till he took his railway hat off. He took us on long rides on the trains. Bobbie and I liked it a lot.

* * *

We got a call one day from North Carolina. Mama told us Daddy had almost died. She said, "I had to walk him all night long around the road and back. After getting over a drunk, his heart almost stopped. I just kept him walking. He had made a promise to God, if only He let him live through this night, he would quit drinking for good. I told him not to promise God anything he does not mean, for God could let him die." After that night, Daddy never drank again. He stopped for good. We all were happy.

I got a call now and then from Lois. She and Richard had bought a house in Alexandria, Virginia so Richard could be close to the Capitol when he worked. Lois would always ask if I was coming back. I missed her and the children so very much. I loved them all.

We had quit the Horn & Hardart's because they were sending us all over the city if they were short of help in another restaurant. We never knew where we would have to work and we wanted to stay in the restaurant where Alex was boss. So we quit.

We both got hired on in an electronics factory in Brooklyn called Lee Springs. We had to sit all day with a soldering iron. We soldered pieces that went into guided missiles. It was an easy job, but you had to do so many a day and you had to solder the pieces just

Mary Judith Messer

right and test them in this testing machine to make sure they worked right.

This boss lady was from Ohio. I don't think she liked me. She sent me to another department downstairs where I met this older man. He was in his forties. He took me out a few times. He was tall with a small mustache. I went to bed with him one time. Then I never saw him again. I didn't even like him and as old as he was, I was crazy to have gone with him. Later I found out he was married. What a jerk and how crazy I was to even go with him.

A good long time after that older man, I told Cheryl I was going to take Bobbie Lee down to this place and have some nice photos taken of him so she can send some to Mama.

We walked down this little hill. There were lots of businesses on both sides of the street. It was just a hop and skip down from 249 Mt. Hope Place, where we lived. I saw the studio, and took Bobbie in.

A man was in. He said, "Hi there. What can I do for you?"

"Take this little fellow's picture," I said. "I would like to know how much it is to have it taken. We want to send some to North Carolina to his grandmother."

"So, you are from North Carolina, from what part?"

He asked every kind of question. Then he said after I answered a dozen questions, "For you, they are free."

I sure was surprised. He then picked up Bobbie and put him on this little table with a white sheet on it. He moved Bobbie's head this way and that. He took lots of photos in different poses.

He said, "Okay, little man," and he lifted him down and put him in a small play room with toys everywhere. He said, "You know what these pictures would cost another person, don't you? Anyone but you would have to pay me two hundred and fifty dollars."

My mouth flew open. "Well, Sir, I am so sorry, but I cannot pay that kind of money. That would take me over three months to work out. I am sorry for your trouble."

He said, "But it costs a lot of money for my film."

"But Sir, you said they were free. How can you take pictures for free, if it costs so much for the film?"

Moonshiner's Daughter

"Look, Judith, the free part I said was for a little favor from you."

"What kind of a favor do you want?" I asked.

He walked over to the door and locked it then came over to me and took me by the hand. "Come on now, you want the free pictures to send to the kid's grandmother, don't you?"

I tried to get away but he had a strong hold on my wrist and he held me on the floor and pulled down my panties. I kicked him and even bit his hand, which he had put over my mouth. He was on me for only a few minutes then off. I jumped up and grabbed my panties but did not put them on. I quickly unlocked the door and rushed to the play room, grabbed Bobbie in seconds and we went out the door with the bells on the door ringing.

He called after me, "Your photos will be ready in a week."

Bobbie fussed all the way home because he wanted to stay in the room full of toys. I didn't tell Cheryl what happened and what a mess I had got myself into. I was so ashamed. When would I ever learn? To this day, every time I see one of those photos, I think about the rape and what a fool I was. That was the second and only other time in New York that I had sex, if you want to call it sex.

Another picture of my nephew, from one of the "walk in" photo booths. This picture never reminded me of the price I paid to have "professional" pictures of him made.

Mary Judith Messer

A Navy Man & Girls In Trouble

About two months later we went to this indoor swimming pool in the Hotel St. George. It was in the dead of winter and freezing outside. We all just loved the pool.

Someone at work told us about the pool so we went to Brooklyn to try it out. We knew Brooklyn pretty well for we were on the subway every morning at six am going to work and we found the hotel just fine. It was a real nice place. We went every chance we got just to play in the water.

We also went to Rockefeller Center to ice skate and I even got me and Bobbie brand new pairs of ice skates. Winter was real cold in New York. The snow would cover the cars it was so deep. It was nice and warm at the electronics factory.

One day we started out after work and saw all kinds of people with these big long trucks and cameras all around. Then someone said, "Hey, that is Jimmy Cagney. He is making a movie here."

I just stood and looked. I just loved the Jimmy Cagney movies. We got a picture of him.

I had met a lot of all kinds of stars and gangsters in New York at the Jack Dempsey Restaurant with Bill. I wished I had got photos of them all. Jimmy also talked to us. It was so nice of him to take time out to talk to a few factory workers like us.

Mama wrote Cheryl a letter and she said that Frederick had been shot and killed. He had taken his gun to this man's house to kill him and the man shot him dead on the front porch.

Cheryl sure was lucky to get away from him. She had good reason to be very afraid of him. Now he was gone, too, like the other man he went to prison for killing.

One Saturday night, I gave all my money to Cheryl. She was to pay Isabella that night for rent and keeping Bobbie. We owed her for two months, around three hundred dollars. Cheryl had it all ready to give Isabella but she was not home when we left the apartment. We had just enough money left over for us a token on the subway and for subway tokens for next week to work and back.

So we took off to the St. George's. I always gave most of my money to Cheryl anyway for safe keeping. We were all in the pool having fun when Cheryl got out and went to the bathroom. Bobbie and I stayed in the pool for over an hour and a half waiting for Cheryl to return. I was getting more worried by the minute. We decided to go look for her.

She was in the lobby with this sailor man. They were just sitting holding hands and all. She said, "Judith, this is John. He is in the Navy."

I could sure see he was in the Navy with that white outfit.

I said, "Why did you not come tell us where you were? We got worried about you when you never came back."

We left her with her friend and went back to the pool. Around 12:30, she came to get us. She said she needed to get Bobbie home in bed.

While we were on the subway, Cheryl said, "Judith, John and I are in love and we are going to be married."

I said, "Boy, that was fast."

Bobbie was asleep on my lap.

She said, "Judith, I let John borrow some money till Tuesday. He is going to meet me Tuesday night at the St. George."

I said, "How much did you let him borrow?"

Mary Judith Messer

She said, "All I had."

I jumped up off the bench and Bobbie hit the floor. "You never gave him all our rent money and baby-sitting money, did you?"

She said, "Don't worry. Tuesday we will get it all back. Plus I will also get a good husband. John loves me."

"My G... Cheryl! What if he does not come back?"

She said, "I know he will be there Tuesday."

"You only met this man tonight! As foolish as I am, I'm not that foolish. You better pray that this John is at the St. George Tuesday night."

We got to the apartment and fell asleep. The next morning Isabella was asking for her money.

Tuesday night, you guessed it. No John, anywhere. Cheryl had talked real sweet to Isabella saying she would get her money for sure Tuesday night.

We waited at the St. George till one-thirty in the morning. He did not come.

Cheryl and I were so upset; we didn't know what to do. She even cried on the way back to our apartment, but it wasn't our apartment for long for when we got to it, a big padlock was on our door.

What in the world to do now with a small kid and no place to lay him down. He was asleep in our arms. We just got on the subway and went to Times Square and 42nd Street. I could not call Bill Donovan. He was in Puerto Rico on business. We just did not know what to do. Not a penny to our name, only a few subway tokens. No food, nothing, and it never crossed my mind to find the YWCA. I was just too upset about how foolish Cheryl had been.

We just walked up and down the sidewalk in Times Square. It was now two am in the morning.

This man saw us and walked over. "Hey, girls. Why are you out this late with the kid? You should have him home in bed. My name isVinny."

Moonshiner's Daughter

He saw that I was almost in tears. We told him everything about getting locked out of our apartment and all.

"Girls, New York is a very dangerous place, especially late at night." Now this Vinny was an older man. He said he was Italian. He seemed like a nice person. He said, "I have a friend, he works in a movie theater in the Bronx."

"The apartment we used to have was in the Bronx, too," I said.

"Well," said Vinny, "you want to go meet him? His name is Bill Bonano. He has a nice apartment. I am sure he will help you girls out."

He flagged down a cab and we got in. We were so relieved to get in a seat. He told the cab driver to take us to a certain movie house in the Bronx. The cab stopped in front of the movie house and Vinny went into the theater. Soon we saw him coming out with a tall, slender, older man. They looked to be about the same age.

Vinny said, "Girls, this is Bill Bonano."

Bill smiled a little and said, "Vinny told me you need a place to stay. Well, I told Vinny to take you to my place a few blocks from here. I will close up and be home later tonight."

The cab and Vinny took us to this pretty nice apartment house. The apartment was on the third floor. Vinny unlocked the door. He said, "You girls put the kid in bed and make yourself at home. Bill will see you later." And Vinny was gone. We never even got a chance to thank him for his help.

Bill said Vinny was a happy married man. He just liked to help people. We never saw Vinny again, but I knew he and Bill got together some for they were good friends.

Bill Bonano was a real nice man. He took us over to our old Italian landlady and talked to her in Italian. He was also Italian like her and like Vinny. He got the key after he paid her every penny we owed her and we went up to get our things out. I sure loved this place.

Bill Donovan was the one that got it for us. I looked at the pretty Chinese wall paper for the last time. I took down all my movie

Mary Judith Messer

star pictures of Natalie Wood, John Wayne, James Dean and Rock Hudson. I had them all up on the bedroom wall. I got them all.

I left the place with a heavy heart. I didn't know what would happen to me. I knew that Bill Bonano liked Cheryl and he wanted her and Bobbie to stay with him. They even were in the same bed when I woke up on the couch the next morning. I was pretty worried anyway. I had not got my period for two months and I was getting more worried. I told Cheryl.

She said, "Who could the father be?"

I had to tell her about the photo man.

She said, "No wonder you made me go pick those pictures up. I wondered why you wouldn't go."

I knew for sure the old man that worked with me at the electronic factory could not be the Daddy. It had been over a year since we were together. Anyway, I could not be sure if I was pregnant but by the next month, I knew for sure I was. Cheryl and I had to tell Bill Bonano. He almost hit the roof.

"Where is that damn man?" he said. He went to hunt him, but had no luck. Bill said, "We will just get Judith an abortion. I know a doctor that can do it."

Cheryl got very afraid I would die. For back then, all kinds of girls that went to have an abortion ended up dead.

She and Bill fought about it.

I was so upset that I did not know what to do. I was making trouble for them and Cheryl was otherwise very happy that Bill didn't want her to work but just to be the house woman.

She had put Bobbie in a good kindergarten for the day. She had lost some weight and had pretty clothing. She had a nice apartment in a real nice part of the Bronx. No more bed bugs.

I never thought Bill Bonano liked me that much, but I was happy for Cheryl. When Bill Bonano was told about Bill Donovan, he said, "Have Judith call him. Maybe he will know what to do with her. I say let her get an abortion."

I sure didn't want to make that call. I was so ashamed. I did not know what to do. I was hoping Bill Donovan would be out of town, but with my luck, he was back in the city. He had a room in one of the big hotels in Manhattan, the Allerton House Hotel. Anyway, I made the call.

"Why, Bunny, I was wondering when you would call. I have been back in New York for three days. I was getting worried when you never called. Where to tonight? How about a play and a good steak restaurant? Sound good to you? I will pick up the tickets. Just name the play."

I tried not to let on anything was wrong, but he said, "What's up? You sound down. Is something wrong?"

I told him all was fine and where to pick me up at 7 pm.

"What's with the new address?" he asked.

"Long story," I said. "I will fill you in tonight."

As soon as Bill Donovan got to the door, Cheryl was waiting for him. She opened the door and Bill was standing there with the big box of candy and a dozen red roses. I tried to get to the door first, but she beat me to it.

Bill Bonano was taking a shower to get ready to go to work at the movie house. Cheryl couldn't wait. She blabbed out to Bill, "I am so glad to see you. You know Judith has got herself pregnant," even before he had time to say hello, let alone give me the flowers and the candy.

Bill Donovan stood and couldn't say a word. Cheryl kept talking her head off. She said, "Bill Bonano, who I live here with, was trying to take her to this doctor to get an abortion…"

Before she got another word out, Bill Donovan said, "No. No way!"

Cheryl said, "What can she do?"

Bill Donovan said, "Don't worry. I will take care of Bunny myself."

We were all standing in the doorway when Bill Bonano came in with his bathrobe on. He walked to the door and said, "Hello. So this is Bill Donovan?"

Bill Donovan didn't even say hello. He reached for my arms and pulled me through the door. He handed the candy and flowers

Mary Judith Messer

to Cheryl. He turned around just to say, "You do not have to worry about Judith. I will see she is taken care of."

Without another word, he took me down in the elevator. "Now Bunny," he said, "this is just life. Things happen. This is not the end of the world. Everything will be fine. You will be fine."

We went to see the play *South Pacific*, on Broadway. He had not changed, not one bit. He was the same old Bill, as always.

After the play, we went to the Stork Club for dinner. While we waited for our meal, he talked to me about life. He told me I would be better off to let someone with a good home give the baby the kind of life I could not give it with a mother and father. He never pressured me to do it, but I could see clearly what he was saying.

Bill was a good person, but he knew I was way too young for him or he may have asked me to marry him. He was more like the father I never had. Looking out for me, he would have done the same for Cheryl also. That was the kind of man he was. I wished a hundred times Cheryl would have went with him. Who knows? She could have married him. He would have been good as gold to her, and he was rich, but now, she had Bill Bonano. They seemed like they really cared for each other even though Bill Bonano was an older man, too.

I told Bill Donovan all about the money and all, for he wanted to know why we gave the apartment up. He had been in Puerto Rico and South America when we needed the money so bad.

The next day Bill came for me and he told Cheryl where he was taking me. He said, "Don't worry for I will check on her a lot."

A happier time in our beautiful apartment before I had to take down all my movie star pictures and move. Notice my poodle skirt!

Mary Judith Messer

A Baby I Loved and A Man I Loved

Bill took me to this Catholic house for unwed pregnant girls. It was behind this big Catholic Church. I was not a Catholic. I was a Baptist, but I never told anyone. I had a room with six other girls all big with babies. All were giving up the babies. The Sisters were good to us, but very strict. No men and if you go out you must be in by 6 pm.

I never liked that place too much, but I tried to make the best of it. Every Sunday, we had to go to Mass. We had to take communion with this white wafer they put on your tongue. We had to go into this small dark booth with a velvet curtain and talk to the priest. We had to tell him everything about our sins, so he could forgive us. I knew only One who could forgive our sins and that was Jesus Christ.

I stayed in that convent for three weeks then Bill took me over to another Catholic convent. I liked it much better. I only had two other girls in my room this time. They were real rich girls from well-to-do families. They had come there so no one would know that they had gotten pregnant. One girl said her parents had told everyone in her hometown she was away at camp. All the girls were giving up the babies. A twelve year old girl was the youngest girl in the convent.

We had a TV Room where we could watch TV anytime, but I never wanted to watch what the other girls were watching. I just stayed in my room or in the sitting room. I never made one friend in the place. I noticed the other girls were not making friends either. We all just kept to ourselves. We had a little kitchen we went into a few at a time, to eat three meals a day. The food was okay. They wanted to make sure we all had healthy babies for them to give to people who wanted babies. I never thought too much about my baby. I just wanted to get myself out of that place.

A Sister Raymond took us all downstairs once a month to get in line, one at a time, to see the doctor. He checked us all out to make sure our babies would be healthy.

Bill Donovan came and picked me up at the downstairs door when he was in town. He took me to Broadway Shows and to a fancy meal. He never came with red roses or candy anymore. I think he didn't want me to put on lots more weight. I was already big as a cow. Bill just came a few more times because he was having to travel a lot with his business.

Cheryl came with Bobbie Lee. We walked over to Central Park. It was only a few blocks from the convent. We walked around in the park. Bobbie looked so nice and clean in his little white shorts and blue shirt. Cheryl was dressed well also. She had lost more weight. Her hair was back to its natural color. She looked better than I had ever seen her. She said she picked out a special school for Bobbie and he liked it.

I sure missed being with them, but from the way Cheryl talked, I started to think that I wouldn't be able to live with Bill Bonano and Cheryl after I had the baby. I did not know what would happen to me. I did not think Bill Bonano wanted me back in his apartment.

I finally went to the hospital to have my baby. They let me see my beautiful little baby girl only one time. I told them I wanted to name her. I named her Brenda Lee after the country music star. I did not know if they put that name on the birth certificate or not. I never got to see one. The hardest thing in my whole life was to sign the adoption paper.

I never knew if my little baby would get a good home or even get adopted. At the convent, we could see down in this alley where all these little boys and girls played. They looked like they were two or three years old and they never had a good home. I worried about little Brenda Lee.

Mary Judith Messer

I was about ready not to sign the papers when Cheryl told me it was best to give the baby a good home and a Mama and a Daddy.

Bill Donovan told me whatever I wanted to do was fine with him, but he also said, "The baby deserves a good life."

I told him about all the little boys and girls playing in the alley everyday with a sister watching them. They had no good home, no happy home. He said, "Bunny, do not worry, your little baby will get a good home. The little children you see were little black children and mixed children. They are very hard to get adopted out. When you first told me about them, I asked Sister Raymond about them before I would let you sign the papers. But whatever you want, you get in the end."

I signed the papers and cried all day.

Bill Donovan asked me, "Would you like to go down to North Carolina for a week or two?"

"Yes, I would like that," I told him. He got me a round trip bus ticket and got me on a bus. He wanted me to fly, but I never liked to fly.

Mama and all were glad to see me. She wondered why Cheryl and Bobbie had not come. She didn't know about the baby and I did not tell her. A few years later, Cheryl told them everything.

I had been back in North Carolina three days when a girl I had known all my life, Julianna Rathbone, paid us a visit. She lived about three houses around Hall Top Road from where Mama and Daddy lived. She asked me to go to town with her. I thought it was a good idea because already I was tired of sitting at the house with the folks.

Julianna and I walked to Waynesville about a mile away, but most of the way was downhill on that old gravel Hall Top Road.

We got to Main Street and walked up and down the street. The town seemed so dead to me after the big city. It was Saturday when everyone was in town for something. I saw the 5 & 10 Cents Store. That brought back bad memories. The old blind man's store was no more. Now, an insurance company was in his building. The town had not changed much from when I was a young girl going into

Moonshiner's Daughter

stores to help Mama steal. A lot of real bad memories came back to me as if it was only yesterday.

In New York, the whole time we lived up there, not one time did I ever think of stealing. It just never crossed my mind and we needed money a lot. We just waited till we could afford to get whatever we needed or borrowed money from friends.

Julianna and I went into the Corner Restaurant on the corner of East Street and Main Street. We got us a seat in a booth where we had a Coke. This place was where a lot of young people hung out. All at once, Julianna called out, "Hey Billy! Come over here."

I saw this young man she was calling to. He walked over to our table and Julianna said, "Judith, this is Billy Wright. Billy, this is Judith Long." I never realized at that time I had just met the love of my life.

Billy was a slender boy and good looking. He was dressed nice in a light colored pair of khaki pants with ironed pleats and also this good shirt. Plus, he was wearing this red light-weight jacket with white trim which I'll always remember.

Julianna asked, "Billy, how about you let me drive that new truck?"

He just reached in his pocket and out came the keys. He said, "Now, I have a full tank of gas. Save me some okay?"

We walked out the door and Billy sat down in our booth. Julianna and I rode all over in his truck. It was a pretty blue Ford. We rode a hundred times up and down Main Street. When the tank of gas was half gone, Julianna and I parked the truck back in front of the restaurant.

I had asked Julianna a thousand questions about this Billy. She also told me the name he went by was William Albert Messer. Messer was his mother's maiden name and he had always gone by that.

When we got back to the restaurant, I went to use the restroom. I later found out while I was in the restroom, William had asked Julianna all kind of questions about me. He even knew where I

Mary Judith Messer

lived. Before he left us in the restaurant to go get his truck filled back up with gas, he asked me out.

Of course I said yes. In all the time in New York, I had never come close to feeling what I was already feeling about William. Of course, I never met many men there, at least not in a good way.

We went out two times. He told me about his stepdad and his mother who hadn't been married when she had him, which was the reason she just used her maiden name for him. He was the only child. He told me everything. He had spent a few years in the Army with an honorable discharge.

I told him goodbye and that I was leaving in two days for New York. He hated to see me go.

I said, "You and Julianna can see each other."

He said, "No, no. We are only friends. I would never go out with her."

William had not even tried to kiss me yet so I didn't think he liked me that much. Back to New York I went.

* * *

Bill Donovan was at the bus terminal when I got there. He was happy to see me.

He said, "Bunny, you sure look rested up. You feel good now?"

I was happy to tell him, "I am great!"

He found me a real nice place to stay in Upstate, New York. I was to live with the Hermans. It was very little housework and a little cooking. I was just doing very simple things for Mrs. Herman. I was to keep her company and do little odd jobs with real good pay. I was also to get free room and board.

Bill Donovan told me to call my sister to let her know I was safe back in town. When I got to the Herman's, I found they were an older Jewish couple. Mrs. Herman was very sick with a bad heart. They both were wonderful people. They were so good to me. The first week, I slept on the couch till they built me a room upstairs, my very own room. The house was real nice and it was on the edge of the golf course. They had a patio I sat on a lot. I had to cook very

little. It was real simple. They gave me a hundred dollars a week.

The Hermans had two grown sons; both were lawyers with wives and two children. Mr. Herman still worked some. It was something to do with all kinds of mixed syrup you put water in to make the best drinks you ever tasted. He had grape, strawberry, orange, just every kind you wanted. You just mixed the syrup with water and you had a great drink.

Mary Judith Messer

About three months after I was at the Herman's, Cheryl called. She wanted me to come to the city and see her and Bobbie.

Mr. Herman took me to catch the train. I told him I would be back before he had to go back to work on Monday. I could hardly wait to tell Cheryl all about the Hermans and my own room they had built just for me.

Cheryl said, "Bill Donovan called me and told us all about the Hermans."

I was happy to see Bobbie. He had grown so much He had this cute little butch haircut. Cheryl told me about news of the city. A lady had been killed next door to her and Bill's apartment house

I talked about the baby and I told her I wished I had never given her up. All she said was the baby would be better off with a nice home, a mother and a daddy. I still cried for little Brenda Lee.

I told her all about William in North Carolina. We talked for hours till she had to go fix supper for Bill Bonano. I spent Saturday and Sunday with them, but I had to catch the train back to the station to the Herman's.

Mr. Herman was waiting for me at the station and I went back to work, sitting with Mrs. Herman. I cooked only light things like some kind of liver. Every day while Mrs. Herman rested, I sat out on the patio under an umbrella and watched the golfers.

Mrs. Herman never came outside. One day after I had been with the Hermans for around six months, the Herman's sons talked the father and the mother into going and putting Mrs. Herman into a home so she would be taken better care of.

I was very sad. I loved the Hermans and I didn't want to have to leave my room.

I called Bill Donovan to tell him the news. He was unhappy also. He said, "Well, Bunny. This is not the end of the world. I will get you another place. I know you do not want to go to Cheryl and Bill's. How would you like to take a trip back home to North Carolina for a few days until I round up another place for you to stay?"

I was glad to take the trip. I had not heard from William since I had come back to New York and I did want to see him again.

Moonshiner's Daughter

A few months after having my baby, I came home at Christmas to see my parents. I may have looked like a "city slicker" but on the inside I was still the "moonshiner's daughter".

I got to mama's house and she said, "William has been coming by a lot. Daddy calls him "Blue Boy" because he drives that pretty blue Ford truck." A man that lived next to my daddy called William "Cigar" because he smoked cigars.

William and I started going together. It was love at first sight to me. He lived with his mother who was quite a bit older and his stepfather.

Bill Donovan wrote me. He said that he would never have thought a country girl turned city girl would return to the country for good, but that was a whole different story.

Cheryl and Bobbie Lee also returned to the mountains again for good. I think she started realizing she didn't want to raise him so far from home.

Bill Donovan came down to Asheville, North Carolina, to see me. He took me out to eat and talk. I told him I was going to get married and he was very happy for me. He told me to write him.

William and I got married, set up a household and had three wonderful sons.

Mary Judith Messer

Finally, back home to NC and married to the love of my life. He was a good man and a good father.

I wrote Bill Donovan about being married and he said, "Bunny, I cannot come back to Asheville. Your husband may come after me with a squirrel gun. Hah! Hah!"

I wrote him about my boys at Easter and he sent them each a bunny. They were beautiful. At Christmas he sent a money order for five hundred dollars. Also he sent three big red wagons called Red Rider. The boys just loved them. We finally lost touch when he moved from the Allerton House Hotel.

What a true friend Bill Donovan was. I left Brenda Lee's hospital papers with him for safe keeping, which I never got back. He may be dead now, I do not know.

* * *

My birth mother was still drinking after I was married, but she finally started going to church and stopped. My birth dad kept making moonshine till he retired but after the night he almost died, and he promised God he would quit drinking if He let him live, he never drank another drop. I do not remember Daddy beating Mama after they all stopped drinking. Daddy had my brother Joe help him in the moonshine business and Joe also went to prison for that when the revenuers arrested him.

Moonshiner's Daughter

When Daddy got too old to tend a still by himself, he showed a young teenage boy how to make the best moonshine that could be made in a copper still. I remember this really skinny fifteen year old kid hanging around my Daddy and his name was Marvin Sutton. My daddy was real mean to Marvin. He made him help him carry all his meal and sugar through the mountains and never gave him a thing other than maybe a pint of moonshine. Later, Marvin got the nickname "Popcorn" and made quite a name for himself as a moonshiner in Maggie Valley and even got on the A & E channel. He made moonshine and drank right at his stills which were my Daddy's. I think he gave them to Popcorn or maybe he just bought them, I don't know. I do know the law has two of my Daddy's and Popcorn's stills. They got Popcorn and the stills and he served jail time lots of times, just like his teacher.

Someone told me that Popcorn said one day, talking about my daddy, "That man was mean as hell but he did give me a good money-making occupation. Without that man, I don't know how I would have turned out."

* * *

And so the story of my early life comes to an end. I was happy now at last with my wonderful husband and three sons, but my heart was still in New York. Not one day passed that I did not think of my Brenda Lee.

I can still see this beautiful pink little baby girl, but only in my dreams is she still a small baby. I hope with my whole heart, before I die, I can see her again if she wants to meet me.

After all these years, Brenda Lee, I need to find you. You were born in the summer of 1958 in Manhattan in a Catholic hospital close to Central Park.

Mary Judith, the Moonshiner's Daughter

Mary Judith Messer

ABOUT THE AUTHOR

Mary Judith Messer was born and raised in Haywood County, North Carolina and ***Moonshiner's Daughter*** is her memoir of growing up in extreme poverty in the Great Smoky Mountains as one of four children born to an abusive moonshiner and his wife. She overcame the handicaps of her upbringing and became a successful business woman, wife and mother of three sons.

Her web site is www.moonshinersdaughter.com. You may order books directly from her or find it at your local bookstore. It is also available on Amazon.com and in e-book versions.